LIVE LIKE YOU GIVE A DAMN

Also by Andrea Owen

*How to Stop Feeling Like Sh*t*
Make Some Noise

Praise for *Live Like You Give a Damn*

"Andrea Owen is the friend you wish your nervous system had growing up. *Live Like You Give a Damn* is clear, actionable, and deeply compassionate—a must-read for anyone ready to get unstuck."

Britt Frank, LSCSW, SEP
licensed neuropsychotherapist and author of
The Science of Stuck and *Align Your Mind*

"If energy is everything, Andrea Owen just handed us the master switch. *Live Like You Give a Damn* is the no-fluff, full-throttle guide to stop dimming, start deciding, and finally live like you actually mean it. This book isn't just a read—it's a recalibration."

Erin King
two-time bestselling author, keynote speaker,
and founder of The Energy Institute

"*Live Like You Give a Damn* is the wake-up call your soul has been waiting for. With Andrea Owen's signature raw honesty and radiant courage, this book gives you a permission slip to trust yourself, speak your truth, and live with unapologetic, heart-led purpose."

Shannon Kaiser
author of *Return to You* and *The Self-Love Experiment*

"*Live Like You Give a Damn* is like sitting down with the most honest, wise friend you've ever had—and realizing that friend is you. Andrea Owen helps you find your voice, honor your truth, and take the empowered action your future self will thank you for."

Terri Cole, MSW, LCSW
psychotherapist, author of *Boundary Boss*
and *Too Much*, and podcast host

"Andrea Owen doesn't just write books—she initiates revolutions. *Live Like You Give a Damn* is a sacred permission slip to stop performing, start feeling, and lead your life like the badass truth-teller you are. This is the new gospel for women who are done pretending and ready to embody their power."

Jessica Zweig
national bestselling author and serial entrepreneur

LIVE LIKE YOU GIVE A DAMN

25 Bold Moves to Get Honest, Face the Hard Stuff, and Show Up for Yourself

Andrea Owen

First published in the US by Sounds True

First published in Great Britain in 2025 by Yellow Kite
An imprint of Hodder & Stoughton Limited
An Hachette UK company

The authorised representative in the EEA is Hachette Ireland,
8 Castlecourt Centre, Dublin 15, D15 XTP3, Ireland (email: info@hbgi.ie)

1

Copyright © Your Kick-Ass Life Coaching, LLC 2025

The right of Your Kick-Ass Life Coaching, LLC to be identified as the Author of the Work has been asserted by them in accordance with the Copyright, Designs and Patents Act 1988.

This book is not intended as a substitute for the medical recommendations of physicians, mental health professionals, or other health-care providers. Rather, it is intended to offer information to help the reader cooperate with physicians, mental health professionals, and health-care providers in a mutual quest for optimal well-being. We advise readers to carefully review and understand the ideas presented and to seek the advice of a qualified professional before attempting to use them.

All names used throughout the book have been changed to protect the privacy of individuals.

Book design by Scribe Inc.

All rights reserved. No part of this publication may be reproduced, stored in a retrieval system, or transmitted, in any form or by any means without the prior written permission of the publisher, nor be otherwise circulated in any form of binding or cover other than that in which it is published and without a similar condition being imposed on the subsequent purchaser.

A CIP catalogue record for this title is available from the British Library

Trade Paperback ISBN 9781399748100
ebook ISBN 9781399748117

Typeset in Sapien

Printed and bound in Great Britain by Clays Ltd, Elcograf S.p.A.

Hodder & Stoughton policy is to use papers that are natural, renewable and recyclable products and made from wood grown in sustainable forests. The logging and manufacturing processes are expected to conform to the environmental regulations of the country of origin.

Hodder & Stoughton Limited
Carmelite House
50 Victoria Embankment
London EC4Y 0DZ

www.yellowkitebooks.co.uk

Contents

	Introduction	1
1	Stop Just Pretending You Want to Change	5
2	Take Responsibility for Your One, Beautiful Life	11
3	Find Your Motivation	19
4	Have a Fierce Throwdown with Fear	29
5	Say What You Mean	35
6	Learn to Parent Yourself	43
7	You Will Disappoint People	51
8	Always Bet on and Choose Yourself	61
9	Keep Your Side of the Street Clean	71
10	How You Do One Thing Is Not How You Do Everything	79
11	You Will Be Handed a Shit Sandwich	87
12	Believe You Were Meant for and Deserve More	95
13	Rush the Net	103

14	People Who Hurt You Can Be Your Greatest Teachers	111
15	Treat Your Trauma with Respect	117
16	People Will Judge You, and Sometimes They're Just Not That Into You	125
17	Be Impractical	131
18	Whatever You Think You Are Will Be Your Truth	143
19	The Big-Wig Boss of Personal Development: Purpose	151
20	You're Not Doing Life Wrong	159
21	Redefine Winning	167
22	Check Your Expectations	175
23	Making Amends Is the Kindest Thing You'll Ever Do	183
24	All You Need Isn't Love, It's Curiosity	191
25	Start Acting Like the Boss of You	199
	Conclusion: This Is What It Means to Give a Damn	207
	Notes	209
	About the Author	211

Introduction

What I'm about to tell you goes against every piece of advice in this book, but hear me out:
Do whatever the hell you want.
If sarcasm is your default communication style, keep it. If ignoring your trauma and flipping off your ex feels more satisfying than facing the pain, go ahead. You're in charge of your life, and nobody—including me—can force you to grow.
Growth is a choice. Healing is a choice. Some people never make that choice, and honestly? That's their call. No one is "bad" for choosing not to evolve. I don't believe everyone is destined for personal transformation in this lifetime.
But here's the deal: Choosing not to grow has consequences. If you don't evolve, your relationships will struggle. If your go-to communication style is passive-aggressive or avoidant, it will create distance, not connection. And if the people around you *are* working on their growth, they will eventually set boundaries with you. When that happens, it's going to feel like rejection. And if you don't understand it for what it is, chaos will follow.

The Power of Chaos

Before you toss this book aside, let's talk about chaos for a moment.
Chaos is often where everything begins. Ancient wisdom from the I Ching says, "Before a person begins a great

endeavor, they may encounter chaos. Out of chaos, brilliant stars are born."[1]

You may have picked up this book in the midst of chaos.

Maybe something inside you is whispering that it's time to change. Maybe you're exhausted from repeating the same patterns. Maybe you're watching your relationships fall apart, your confidence take a hit, or your self-trust erode.

That's where this book begins: with the messiness of figuring out what it means to *live like you give a damn*.

Who This Book Is For

This book is for people who are ready to embrace a little chaos in the name of change.

Let's be clear: This isn't about becoming a different person. You're not here to turn into some enlightened leader who never loses their shit. This is about:

- Making conscious choices instead of living on autopilot.
- Recognizing your patterns and asking, *Is this really serving me?*
- Learning how to shift those patterns in a way that actually sticks.

I've spent years working with women who thought they were "too broken" or "too set in their ways" to change. Here's what I know for sure: You're never too anything to choose differently.

The women I work with aren't special unicorns with supernatural abilities to transform their lives. They're regular people who *decided* that living like they give a damn was worth the temporary discomfort of growth.

What You'll Get from This Book

Each chapter tackles a specific challenge, breaking it down into three parts:

1. **What the problem is**—so you can see how it's showing up in your life.
2. **What happens if you don't address it**—because ignoring it won't make it go away.
3. **How to "fix" it**—with practices, tools, and strategies you can start using right now.

You don't have to read this book cover to cover. You can skip around. Pick a chapter that speaks to you and start there. If a topic resonates, lean into it. If it doesn't, move on.

But here's my promise to you: If you show up with curiosity, a willingness to get a little uncomfortable, and maybe even laugh at yourself along the way, you'll come out of this process more connected to yourself and the life you want to live.

Why You Should Listen to Me

I know this because I've been there.

I've been the queen of chaos—the one who used sarcasm as armor and wine as a shield. My own journey started almost twenty years ago when my first marriage imploded and I found myself alone, realizing that my go-to coping mechanisms weren't cutting it anymore.

That wake-up call led me down a path I never expected—from desperately seeking answers to becoming the person who helps others find theirs.

For the past seventeen years, I've worked with thousands of women, written multiple books, and created spaces where we can get real about what it means to actually show up for our lives.

My books have been translated into twenty languages, reaching women around the world. My podcast, *Make Some Noise* (which has over five million downloads) is where I've had conversations with hundreds of the best experts in personal development.

I've stood in the chaos, wondering if the hard work was worth it.

It always is.

So, if you're ready to dive in, let's embrace the chaos together and figure out what it means for you to live like you give a damn.

1

Stop Just Pretending You Want to Change

You wouldn't have picked up this book unless you wanted some kind of change in your life. Maybe you're going through a transition and want to feel more alive—that the past has left you taking care of everyone else and now it's your turn. Or you know there's something more out there and all the skin-care products in the world aren't filling the gaping hole you feel in your spirit. Or perhaps you dabble in personal development, hoping *This Book* will finally be the one that changes your life. Well, guess what? It can, but it won't. Let me explain.

When I was in my twenties, I picked up the book *Don't Sweat the Small Stuff* by Richard Carlson. I loved reading it, and the bite-size chapters of wisdom were just what I needed as both a young woman and a personal development newbie.

After that, I filled my bookshelf with books that my therapist or a wise, older friend suggested, or if something caught my eye in the bookstore. But the truth is, when I would read these books, many times only half reading them, I thought it all sounded good, and I liked the *idea* of changing for the better, but I was nowhere near a place where I would take action. I even wrote the names of my friends and boyfriends in the margins of these self-help books because I was clear *they* needed to change, but not me. Not only this, but I was also convinced that my life would be better if the other people in my life would implement the changes I was reading about in these smart books. I, on the other hand, could and would remain the same.

What Happens If You Keep Just Pretending You Want to Change?

Pretending you want to change is like staring at a locked door while holding the key in your hand. It might feel productive to read another book, share another inspirational quote, or say, "I'm working on it," but deep down you know you're stalling. Staying in this limbo is deceptively comfortable—it lets you fantasize about a better life without requiring you to face the vulnerability, risk, and effort of actual change. I know this because I've been there.

As I filled my bookshelf with self-help books, I became convinced they'd fix everything without me actually doing the work. I loved the thought of change, but I wasn't ready to face the action it required. And that's exactly what happens when you keep pretending: You admire the idea of transformation from a safe distance, but nothing actually shifts.

When you keep pretending, you risk growing resentful—of yourself, others, and even the tools meant to help you. I blamed my circumstances for why change wasn't happening: *I'm too busy, I don't have the support, it's not the right time*. But deep down, I knew the truth—I wasn't ready to face the work. And let me tell you, that dissonance between who you *are* and who you say you want to be is suffocating. I was stuck, and the only person keeping me there was me.

The real cost of pretending, though, isn't just frustration or stagnation. It's the erosion of trust in yourself. Every time you say you're going to change but don't, you chip away at your confidence and your belief in your own ability to follow through. That cycle can leave you feeling like change isn't possible for you, convincing you to settle for less than what you truly want.

So, if you're still pretending, ask yourself this: How much longer are you willing to stay stuck? At what point will the discomfort of staying the same outweigh the fear of taking action? Because here's the thing—I know how scary it is to step into the unknown. But I also know that change is so much less terrifying than staying in that familiar, stagnant place where nothing ever shifts. The books, the quotes, and the affirmations won't save you. Only you can do that. And the moment you decide to stop pretending is the moment you start truly living.

How to Actually Change Your Life

In order to change your life, real action is required, far beyond reading words on a page. This might seem obvious, but it's crucial that you understand a few things before you dive into changing your life.

People often miss the imperative first step, the grand hoo-hah if you will, and that's deciding on and setting the intention to change. People think about it, admire from afar those who create shifts, look around a bit more, and kick some "transformation tires." But, sadly, nothing happens.

Then there are the people who will likely remain miserable their whole lives. They won't solve manageable problems because the attention they get from having these problems gives them more satisfaction than solving the problem. (My guess is this isn't you, but you can now scrawl someone's name in the margins.)

Does any of this describe you? Are you just pretending you want to change? Are you comfortable being known for having certain persistent problems and are fine with that?

If it is, honestly, that's okay; just know that's where you are. It's better to be sincere with yourself that even though you may *want* to change and better your life, you're not yet willing or ready to accept the action it takes to transform. Everyone has their own pain tolerance of how much bullshit they can take in their life before they take steps to move away from it—no one but you can tell you what your tolerance threshold is. You might be at a place where you haven't reached that threshold yet. Don't worry, you'll get there eventually.

However, when you do make that decision, you'll likely be fearful of what's to come. That's normal. But I'll bet all the money and magic beans in the world that what might come during your metamorphosis is less scary than staying where you're at—the place that you're sick and tired of being in.

Changing and bettering your life will be one of the most uncomfortable and difficult things you'll ever do. It requires you to look inward at all the ways your thoughts, beliefs, and patterns are not great (and sometimes just plain shitty). Changing and bettering your life *demands* that you dig into your darkness. It will compel you to move away from things and people—like a crab scurrying sideways—even though you've become comfortable with these things and people... but they're actually pulling you down.

Transforming your life in a positive direction will challenge you in ways you've probably never faced before, requiring you to find a new ferocity for yourself you didn't know was possible.

The biggest and most important question you need to ask yourself: *Do I want to change my life as much as the work entails?*

In other words, are you absolutely sure you're willing to put in the effort, emotions, and energy it takes to better your life? Are you prepared to dedicate the time and humility that self-examination will take in order to change? Are you at a place where you are more uncomfortable with where you're at versus the discomfort of changing (that, may I remind you, hasn't taken place yet, so you don't know how uncomfortable it will be)? And lastly, do you have the patience for the journey and know that it will take your whole life—that in order to get through that journey, you'll need to honor and trust the process?

I encourage you to get out the note-taking app on your phone, one of the many journals you've purchased when you knew this was the time you were going to change your life, or even a cocktail napkin to answer those questions. And yes, I'm making it sound like this is some kind of secret "It's Your Life Fight Club," because, well, it is.

READY, AIM, PLAN

So, you're at that "ready" place—you've stopped just pretending you want to change. Hooray! Next comes your intention.

Intention setting is about stating what you're about to do as well as committing to the process. Write it out, put it on a sticky note, scrawl it in lipstick across your bathroom mirror, post on social media about it—whatever you need to do that feels like a solid intention. If you're stuck, here are some questions to get you started. Be specific when you answer:

- What do you want more of in your life?
- What matters most to you?
- What do you want or need to let go of?
- When are you the proudest of yourself?
- What's next for you that's in service of your highest self?
- Who are you becoming?

You might get broad, substantial answers to these questions, and that's great. For example, if you answered "peace" for the question about what you want more of and answered "drama" for what you want less of, now get more specific. What does that look like in your life? Who are the people or circumstances involved? What are the realistic steps that need to happen in order to get you from where you are now to where you want to go?

Next come the small steps. Do you want to move on from your destructive former relationship and start dating again? Start researching therapists and make an appointment. Do you want to change careers? Look into what needs to happen, make a list, and start small today. Do you need to set boundaries in order to get more peace and have less drama? Get a book on the topic and start taking notes on how to have those tough conversations. This isn't rocket science. *It's about getting clear that you want to do things differently and being purposeful about it* by setting your intention and coming up with small action steps that will add up over time.

This is your life. There are no refunds, even if you just give it one out of five stars. You've been bestowed the beautiful gift of agency, free will, and the desire to improve your future. No one can do it but you, and that's good news because no one else will do it as phenomenally as you. In order to change your life, you actually have to *change your life*. Go in slowly, or get after it with ferocity, whichever you choose. But no matter what, the greatest part is you're choosing yourself, and that's the best course of action you can take.

2

Take Responsibility for Your One, Beautiful Life

I tend to work with a decent number of anxious people. They begin their work with me excited about changing their lives, and ready to do it, but many times what brings them to this point is their unease about where they currently are in their lives and where they're headed.

Whenever I work with a new client, they fill out an intake packet full of questions that help us get started. The dozen or so powerful inquiries range from "What is the one thing in your life right now that is causing you the most discomfort or stress?" to "In terms of working together, what would a successful experience look like?"

The answers vary from client to client, as each person is unique. However, there is a prevalent theme to one particular question: When I ask, "What is standing between where you are now and the person you want to be?" almost every single client answers, "Me."

They go on to say something about the fact that they know they are in their own way but that they just can't seem to get past their own obstacles to get to where they want to go. The great thing about this answer is that when people know and admit this, it says they're ready to take responsibility for their one, beautiful life. Once you have the awareness around being your own obstacle, you're then able to work on moving past it.

But... what does "getting in your own way" even mean?

In its simplest terms, getting in your own way happens when you are impeding your own progress or success by your thoughts, beliefs, feelings, and actions. I've yet to meet a person who doesn't do this at some point or another—it's a universal experience, and again, the key first step is to realize that you're doing it.

What Happens If You Don't Embrace Responsibility for Your Life?

Not sure if this is you? Here are some additional specific ways of what it looks like to get in your own way.

Negative Self-Image and Chronic Negative Self-Talk

Having a negative self-image and exercising chronic negative self-talk are related and somewhat of a chicken/egg scenario, although it really doesn't matter which one came first. What matters is if they both exist for you. You might undermine your abilities and accomplishments, therefore undercutting your self-confidence. You might beat yourself up for mistakes. Or perhaps you have too-high expectations of yourself, so you are bound to fall short and never cut yourself any slack.

Having a Fear of Failure

Having a fear of failure—and even a fear of success—prevents you from taking any risks. Most of us have some varying fear of failure that we know about. If we go down what I like to call "seven layers deep," the fear of failure equals the fear of shame. What we define as failure has a much heavier charge to it than simply being embarrassed. When we see ourselves as failures or even our behavior that led to the defeating event as a failure, the emotional impact can leave an imprint long after the event has passed.

The fear of success is the sneaky, lesser-known sister of the fear of failure. It's that subtle, often overlooked hesitation that keeps us from stepping into what's possible for us. Sometimes we get in our own way by being afraid of success, what that success will mean to us, and how it will impact us. We might worry about the added responsibilities, the changes in our relationships, or even the pressure to maintain that success. It's as if we're standing on the edge of greatness but something inside holds us back, whispering doubts about whether we can handle what's on the other side.

Procrastination and/or Self-Sabotaging

To be fair, procrastination and self-sabotaging can also stem from neurodivergence and, at times, trauma (more on that in chapter 15). Regardless, these two habits make it difficult to do things like keep up with our to-do lists and goals. They quickly become behaviors that we sometimes end up blaming on our personality, zodiac sign, or "things that make us quirky."

Striving for Perfection

Trying to attain perfection can keep you stuck in "analysis paralysis." This can mean you either don't start anything new for fear it won't be perfect or you don't finish much, constantly thinking it needs more work in order to live up to unrealistic expectations put on it by you.

Overthinking

Overthinking past decisions, things you have no control over, or past or future scenarios is common for my anxious audience. (Hi, me too!) By creating a cycle of indecision and nervous energy, you stay stuck and in your own way. It's like being on a mental hamster wheel, exhausting yourself without actually getting anywhere. This constant rumination not only drains your energy but also prevents you from taking meaningful action. Recognizing this pattern is crucial to understanding how it hinders your progress.

Questioning Your Abilities or Second-Guessing Yourself

Questioning your abilities or second-guessing yourself gets in your way by leading to a lack of confidence that keeps you from pursuing new opportunities. It's like standing at the edge of a diving board, knowing you can swim but hesitating to take the plunge. This self-doubt can paralyze you, making you hesitate to step out of your comfort zone. Over time, it becomes a barrier to growth, preventing you from embracing challenges that could lead to personal and professional development.

Chronic Pessimistic Thinking

We all go through bouts of pessimistic thinking. It's completely normal to sometimes think negatively or be convinced things are too hard or won't work out. But when it becomes a chronic habit, things tend to go sideways.

Blaming Others

Of course, some people do things that upset us and impact our lives negatively; this isn't about letting them off the hook. There's a difference between being upset that someone has harmed you and then eventually moving on, versus staying stuck in the blame and using that as an excuse to stay where you are and not move forward. This can lead to picking arguments and finding fault in everyone's behavior around you. It develops into a cycle of looking for evidence that you are the victim in everything, and then it becomes an easy way to stay stuck and disempowered.

Putting Your Happiness Eggs in Someone Else's Basket

What tends to happen over time into adulthood is that we put our happiness and fulfillment onto the to-do list of other people or things. We think the right partner will fulfill us completely, and they don't. We think the best job will make all our dreams come true, and it doesn't. The list continues to things like having children, the perfect amount of money, and the shape of our bodies and appearance. We think these milestones will magically transform us, and they might for a bit. But once that initial excitement wears off, we're back to being in the reality of our lives.

Whether you relate to one of these behaviors of getting in your own way or all of them, taking complete responsibility for your life will end up getting you an enormous sense of freedom and empowerment. Let's look at how to do it.

How to Take Responsibility for Your Life

If any of those habits above that I mentioned are habits you partake in, I'll say it again like I'll say it one hundred times: You're normal. You've created coping mechanisms based on avoiding judgment, shame, failure, and criticism, and you've probably done a decent job at it. However, all of those things block you from being your best self and living like you give a damn.

By admitting the specifics of where you get in your own way, you push your ego aside and can begin to take accountability. The only people who change their ways to be able to find the happiness and contentment they're looking for are people who do this. But it's vulnerable, and it takes a giant swallowing of your pride. I'll break it down into four parts: practicing self-awareness, dropping excuses, limiting your limiting beliefs, and setting goals.

Practice Self-Awareness

So, let's get real about taking charge of your one, beautiful life. First up, self-awareness. Think of it as your personal GPS—without it, you're just driving in circles, wondering why you keep ending up at the same dead end. Start tuning in to your thoughts and behaviors without judgment, only curiosity (we'll cover this more in chapter 24). Journaling or a bit of meditation can help you spot those pesky patterns that trip you up. By documenting your thoughts and feelings, you can identify recurring themes and triggers, gaining valuable insights into your inner world.

Drop Those Excuses

Next, be conscious of your excuses. Some of them are warranted, like if you're a single mom with little to no help, trying to get your business up and running, and it's proving to be difficult. But sometimes your excuses are just BS, fear, or self-sabotage. For example, if your partner wants you to go to couples counseling with them to deal with your relationship issues and you say no, that you don't have time for that because you have to go to the gym every day after work, that's not okay. Changing your life requires you to be vulnerable, probably the most vulnerable you've ever been. That vulnerability starts with looking at your excuses and getting honest about which ones are legit and which ones aren't.

Limit Your Limiting Beliefs

Now let's make awkward eye contact with those limiting beliefs (we'll cover this in chapter 18). They're like that outdated software slowing down your mental operating system. Time for an upgrade! For example, if you tell yourself, *I'll never find true love* or *It's too late for me*, I invite you to challenge these beliefs by asking, *Is this fact or just fiction I've been telling myself?* Swap out *I can't handle this* for *I'll try my best at this* and watch your mindset slowly shift. Thought shifts and visualization techniques can reinforce these empowering beliefs, helping you rewire your brain for positive thinking.

If you're new to visualization, start simple. Close your eyes and take a few deep breaths to relax. Now picture yourself achieving something you want—maybe it's nailing a big presentation, confidently setting a boundary, or feeling peaceful in a stressful situation. Engage all your senses—what do you see, hear, or feel in that moment? Imagine the confidence in your posture, the ease in your voice, the feeling in your body, or the joy of accomplishment. The key is to make it as vivid as possible, like a mental movie. Practice this daily for a few minutes. Over time, your brain starts to associate those positive feelings with real-life actions.

Set Some Goals

Lastly, onto goal-setting. Set clear, achievable goals—like tackling those limiting beliefs you just read about, or any of the tools and strategies you'll read about in the upcoming chapters. Break them down into bite-size steps and celebrate each little win. It's like giving yourself a high five for adulting. This approach not only makes large goals more attainable but also builds momentum and confidence.

Taking decisive action is crucial. Procrastination is like binge-watching a show you don't even like but hoped would get better—it's a time-suck. Commit to action, even when it's tiny or uncomfortable. Start with small tasks to build confidence, and soon you'll be tackling bigger challenges like a pro. Overcoming procrastination involves recognizing the underlying fears and addressing them head-on. (See chapter 4 for more on procrastination.)

By weaving these strategies into your life, you're setting yourself up to move past self-imposed roadblocks and create a life that's authentically yours. Remember, taking responsibility is the first step to living like you give a damn and cannot be skipped. And it's an ongoing journey that requires patience, persistence, and a good sense of humor.

3

Find Your Motivation

When I was about to graduate from college, I was thirty-four and eight months pregnant with my second child. I had taken the long way to finish my degree—starting with junior college at the age of eighteen, where I had then flunked out. I went back to school years later and pulled up my GPA from a 1.7 while I trudged through a terrible divorce, then dated a con man, got pregnant with my first child, then got remarried. So there I was, mostly settled down, having my second baby and about to graduate with honors with a degree in exercise physiology.

I sat opposite my advisor in her small office, bookshelves bulging with textbooks, sunlight streaming through the tiny window high above her head. After everything I had been through to get there and graduate, I was excited to tell her my career plans.

With a cheerful voice I announced, "I'm going to pursue becoming a certified life coach and bring my knowledge of fitness and health science there."

But my excitement was not met by her.

She chuckled, gave me a forced smile, waved her hand, and said, "But... can you make any money doing that? Seems like a waste of your education."

I felt like I was seven years old and getting scolded by one of my parents, which felt even worse given that this advisor was my age. As most of my peers were off to grad school or becoming physical therapists or athletic trainers for college or even professional teams, there I was off to be a life coach. I felt small, stupid, and humiliated. She had looked at me as if I told her my plan was to make a six-figure career of dressing up as a clown and making balloon animals for my imaginary friends.

I left her office head down, feeling defeated and angry.

Soon after that meeting, I realized I had been underestimated, which is a terrible feeling but also one of the many ways we can be motivated—though not the typical "right" way.

What Happens If You Don't Find Your Motivation?

Doing a Google search for "motivational videos" yields 167 million hits. There is no shortage of books, keynote speakers (waves cheerfully), podcasts, and sports posters with epic quotes on them that will likely inspire you, but you'll be swimming in *meh* until you understand specifically what motivates you. None of it really matters until you see this clearly and run with it.

Before I put on my professional hype-girl hat, we need to first discuss some things that will sap your motivation. These are unsexy but must be talked about because you might be trying to push a boulder up a hill when it comes to getting pumped up and staying motivated.

First, a motivation squasher that doesn't get talked about enough is heartbreak. I can't tell you how many clients I've had who get down and out about not accomplishing their goals while they were simultaneously walking through a challenging and sometimes complete shitstorm in their life, such as a rocky relationship or marriage, being a new empty nester, or having a pet or loved one die within the last year or so.

Heartbreak is a motherfucker; it will flip you upside down and shake you out even when you're not expecting it. This type of unhappiness has no real timeline and can leave us feeling like we don't have any control over the situation. Even the pandemic was an uncomfortable kind of sadness, a wet blanket of sorts. When we don't surrender to these feelings and give them space, it settles in for the long haul, like a tick behind your ear you didn't know was there, sucking the blood from you and making you sick. Honor your heartbreak, sadness, or other feelings of discomfort, whatever they are, or they will stick around longer and drag you down.

Also, if you're in any kind of heartbreak—even if you're "having a hard time"—make sure you're not beating yourself up for not feeling that spark for the things you want to accomplish. Motivation requires space, both mental and emotional, and when that space causes you to hit the brakes, you need time to settle back into a prime zone for putting your foot on the gas pedal and forging ahead.

While heartbreak can and will sideline your motivation, the big cheese of motivation killers is fear, and no one escapes this one. Fear of failure: whether it's remembering past failures or making up future ones, fear of what others think or may think, fear that you won't follow through or that you will and then won't be able to sustain it; fear of getting it wrong, fear of not knowing where to start, fear of clowns. Practically anything can find a way to be a fear when it comes to something important to you that you need motivation around. The more meaningful to you it is, the more likely fear will worm its way in and be an obstacle.

COMBATING FEAR

There are countless ways to combat fear, but when it comes to bypassing it to specifically get your mojo back, I'll break it down into five steps in the form of questions. The key here is to get curious and unpack your thoughts and beliefs around your fear so that you can move through it and create new beliefs and behaviors. I encourage you to get out a piece of paper or your journal of choice and answer the following questions for yourself:

- **Pinpoint the fear and where it came from.** You have to name it to tame it, but not only that. What's its origin story? Was it handed down to you from a parent, from a past experience, or is the fear completely made up?
- **How likely is it that this fear will actually happen?** Think with your logical self on this one, not your anxious self. On a scale of 1 to 10, how likely is it that you'll fail? Or that others will judge you? Often it's not that likely, but if it is . . .
- **If one of your fears does happen, how likely is it that you'll be able to manage it?** For instance, if it doesn't work out the way you want it, can you learn from it and try again? If others have negative comments about it, can you hear them and move forward anyway? Following the thread and thinking through each scenario with a growth mindset and positive outlook can put out the fire of fear that's raging in your mind.
- **Ask yourself if the pain of not going after your goals is greater than your fear.** Imagine yourself ten or twenty years from now, having not gone after your goals because your fear was too hefty to do it. Is that acceptable to you? Or do you

want to look back and know that your goal, your dream, your life was bigger than your fear? That you—the capable, resourceful, badass human that you are—were able to manage and make your way through your apprehension to get to the other side?

- **How can you use your fears as fuel to push you through?** This can be one of the single best ways to shore up motivation. Afraid you'll fail? Decide that even if you do, failure is a necessary step to get to where you're going. Nervous of others' opinions? Understand that their negative opinions are simply their own fears projecting onto you and not your problem to deal with. Most fears can be pushed through by changing your mindset around the thought. Use the energy that the fear is taking up and convert it to ammunition to sustain you through to your goal.

To regain your mojo, examine your fear with curiosity. Identify its origin, assess its likelihood, and consider if you could handle it. Weigh the pain of inaction against your fear—will you regret not trying? Finally, use fear as fuel, reframing failure as growth and ignoring others' doubts. Shifting your mindset helps you push through and move forward.

How to Find Your Unique Brand of Motivation

In terms of "appropriate" ways to be motivated, let's talk about intrinsic motivation, or what I like to call the things you do because you give a shit about them. In fact, you'd still do them if no one knew anything and you received no feedback about it from others. Your actions align with your values and interests, make you feel like you, and these are the things you're passionate about.

For example, you may be an activist for saving the environment, and your motivation comes from your deep belief that as humans, it's our responsibility to do so. You do it for no other reason except that it feels wrong for you not to take action.

Intrinsic motivation is often the kind that people rely on who feel as though they have a life purpose—like becoming a surgeon, running for office, or opening a rescue for disabled cats and dogs. The bottom line here is that this is important to you, and if it's not important to anyone else, that doesn't hinder how you feel about it or the action you take.

Next, and what I want to focus the rest of this chapter on, is extrinsic motivation, which are the things that come from outside of us.

Extrinsic motivation often gets a bad reputation. Some experts say you should only find your motivation from within. While of course that's always an exceptional and ideal way to be motivated, let's be honest: As humans, we care considerably what other people think, even if we can win an Academy Award for acting like we don't. So let's get our motivation where we can and go from there.

One type of extrinsic motivation is to be motivated by pleasure or pain. This could include seeking out getting good grades because your parents validated you for that; getting a promotion because of the status and money it brings; or continuing to have sex with someone you know will always remain a "situationship" because the sex is epic and keeps you coming back, even if what you actually desire is a long-term partnership. All of these examples of extrinsic motivation can also be looked at through the lens of being fear motivated. The student who doesn't want to get anything less than A's because they fear disapproval or not being a part of a social circle they want to remain in. Not getting that promotion can make a person feel shame. Walking away from your situationship can make you feel unloved and like no one pays attention to you. We are often motivated by a mix of pain, fear, and pleasure. The point is, fear-based motivation isn't necessarily a problem—unless it's leading you away from what you truly want rather than toward it.

Another form of extrinsic motivation is setting goals to try to impress people. I don't care if you know when you're doing this or not; we all do it, and being motivated by trying to look good and awe others is at least part of the equation. As I just mentioned, as humans we care about what other people think of us, so instead of focusing on only impressing yourself, how about you set goals that you want to set and simply notice if you're doing it to impress others? It's going to happen sometimes regardless, so take a nonjudgmental look at how much that's fueling your motivation. If you realize it's solely to make yourself look good in front of your family, friends, or the internet, maybe it's time to rethink your goals.

Or not.

Sometimes the juicy lesson you need comes from following through on the goal and paying attention to how you feel when you get there. Do you feel a giant *thunk* at the end, a hollowing out of your spirit because the success doesn't bring you what you thought it would? Maybe then it's time to acknowledge that your goal is about impressing others. Perhaps it's time to look at any people-pleasing or perfectionism issues you have. Those examples could be the underlying problem, but many times it takes following through on the poor source of motivation or unhealthy coping mechanism for you to look at it for what it is and make changes.

***

Getting back to my college advisor's office and the mildly humiliating experience of being underestimated. Many of the people in my community, including my readers, are women. For women, and in terms of motivation, being underestimated can be a big deal and can do one of two things.

It can either take you down in one swift motion, where you take to heart the person who underestimated you and believe them when they question your abilities—thus validating your own inner critic and negative self-talk. It can add to the already full (shit)pile of evidence you've been collecting that you're not good enough, smart enough, creative enough, whatever enough. It can pull you into a place where you dismiss and walk away from your goals and dreams, and then you make decisions about your life based on that person's assumption and shortsighted opinion.

For many of us, it's not a single person who underestimates us but an entire culture. We are, as women, often the underdog by default, and this is especially true for women in marginalized communities.

But being underestimated can be used as an accelerant to light a fire within you so enormous it could take down that person's or our culture's shortsighted opinion. That inferno could be considered your baptism into your biggest motivation.

Your choice.

After that fateful meeting, I spent some time feeling like I was wrong for making the decision to become a life coach. I worried my advisor might be right, that I might be destined to be destitute. As time went on, I not only changed my perspective on that but realized that being underestimated was not new to me and it had the opportunity to be my biggest motivator.

Over a decade later, I still use being underestimated as one of my biggest sources of motivation, but only to fuel me in regard to goals that are truly important to me. In other words, it's an accessory motivator: intrinsic motivation is the foundational ensemble, but being underestimated makes the outfit amazing.

In the end, when you are finding motivation to accomplish goals that someone else has put on you or goals that you think you "should" have but mean nothing to you, eventually that's going to feel like trying to put toothpaste that's been smeared all over the mirror back into the tube. It will leave you frustrated and possibly make you angry in the process; not to mention it's impossible. But . . . it might work for a little while.

Sooner or later, as you learn more about yourself and evolve as a person, it will become imperative to pick goals that you truly give a shit about, that are aligned with who you are or want to be, and that are going to make you feel like a billion bucks (because we all know in this economy, it's a billion now). No matter how you get there.

4

Have a Fierce Throwdown with Fear

In 2016, shortly after my father passed away, I got the word *surrender* tattooed on my forearm in my own handwriting.

The fear I had surrounding the grief I went through after his death was all-consuming. I was afraid of the experience of that level of grief—worried it would swallow me whole, that I'd never stop crying, and that if I let it in, my heart would break so violently it would kill me.

Dramatic, right?

Fear will do whatever it needs to do to keep you in it. In my case, specifically around being lost in a new emotional experience of losing a loved one, my fear was working overtime making up stories about what might happen if I surrendered to the grief. So, I hitched a ride with those fear stories and didn't look back.

Until I had to look back.

Before I tell you about that crash and burn, let me make it clear that not all fear is bad. Our body and brain communicate quickly when real fear is present. For example, when someone who looks like they might be dangerous approaches us, when we're driving in a bad storm without much experience in doing so, or when we're alone with someone we have a history of negative experiences with—there are situations that warrant our precious fear response. But more often than not, our fears are triggered when they don't need to be. In many of those instances, the way fear shows up isn't as obvious as you might think.

Three insidious ways fear manifests in our lives and prevents us from growing are resistance, procrastination, and negative self-talk.

Resistance and procrastination are like parent and child, respectively. Resistance gives birth to procrastination in that we want to start or change something, and we fear that change for a myriad of reasons. From there, procrastination saunters in looking cute. We put off and postpone actions that will ultimately benefit us because we feel more comfortable there. Resistance then wins.

Negative self-talk is also there, telling us we shouldn't do "the thing," that we're too late, we're too inexperienced, we might fail, we might succeed and won't be able to sustain it. For the grand finale: *What will people think?*

These three behaviors and mindsets collude with each other and become a strong force in your mind, making you feel cozy there. And the cycle repeats.

What Happens If You Don't Challenge Your Fears?

In *The War of Art*, Steven Pressfield describes resistance as the force that keeps people from pursuing their true potential. He explains that most people live two lives—the one they actively live, and the one they dream of living. Resistance is what stands between the two, manifesting as self-doubt, procrastination, and avoidance. It's the reason people abandon personal goals, creative endeavors, or meaningful callings. Pressfield emphasizes that deep down, everyone knows the work they are meant to do, yet resistance keeps them from acting on it, making excuses and delaying progress indefinitely.[1]

We get something from that resistance. Of course we would, or we'd abandon the resistance as soon as we realize it's happening.

Resistance allows us to stay safe. It allows us to avoid any risk, vulnerability, judgment, exposure, or getting it wrong. Resistance is the main character in our fear stories.

Procrastination

As I mentioned before, procrastination is the devilish spawn of resistance—a symptom of fear and resistance. Procrastination does not mean that you are lazy or stupid. It's simply a behavior we employ to get what we want: comfort and ease in the present moment.

If we want to go deeper, we can't overlook our emotions. Timothy A. Pychyl, the author of *Solving the Procrastination Puzzle*, talks about how procrastination isn't a problem of time management but rather emotional management. We have feelings about the things we're resisting and thus procrastinating on, and then we have more feelings about the procrastination we engage in. His research argues that if we can learn to manage our emotions around the tasks at hand, we'll be better about forming habits to take the action we ultimately want to do.

Negative Self-Talk

Negative self-talk, or the "inner critic," is the consequence and expression of resistance and procrastination. It's the voice in our head that beats us up for even thinking we could complete our task or goal, for putting things off, for "looking stupid," and so on. The more unaware you are of this voice, the more likely you are to have it. Whether you know it's there or not, it's sure to make you feel like shit.

I go in-depth on this topic in my book *How to Stop Feeling Like Sh*t* and the audio program *Getting Damn Good at Life*, but for the sake of this chapter, let's start with your awareness here. Do you notice that your inner critic gets louder when you're thinking about or planning big goals? If so, that's common. You can now use that as a signal that you're on to something big. Our inner critics reserve their chatter for these times in our lives—where there's a lot at stake.

How to Have a Fierce Throwdown with Fear

As always, the first step to having a fierce throwdown with fear is self-awareness, which you're already strolling through, taking the time and attention to read this chapter.

Steps 1 and 2: Identify and Get Clear on Your Fear

First, you must get intimate with fear—get into the kitchen with it in order to know your unique recipe and understand how it operates backward and forward. At this point in your life, you have an established set of patterns of behavior that are particular to you.

Steps 1 and 2 are about getting clear on what your unique "method for the madness" is and then challenging the stories within that. Here are some examples. Do you get lost in the comparison trap especially, getting triggered by coworkers, friends, strangers on the internet? Do you quickly and easily feel insecure and small based on the perceived lives of others? If yes, identifying that is your step 1.

Step 2 would be to start paying attention to the nitty-gritty here. Is it worse during certain times of your menstrual cycle? Or with certain people or places? Does social media exacerbate this? Get curious without judgment. Writing out these things or journaling on them can help.

Or maybe your fear is based on a lack of self-confidence. Deep down you don't believe you can accomplish big things. It's too hard, you're not smart enough, you're not ready, you're simply convinced you can't do it. If this is you, again, get curious. What about the story convinces you of this? Where is there any clear proof it won't work? What specific stories are you making up and believing about this?

Or perhaps your fear is rooted in what others might think. You're afraid of their opinions of your goals, afraid of failing or even just struggling in front of others, afraid of the attention if you succeed; or you're just generally cowering at the thought of others' judgment. If this is your recipe, I invite you to start with compassion for yourself here. You're human; of course you're worried about what others think. The real fear here is of shame, and your brain is simply trying to protect you. Now that you know this, write out—with kindness—all of the possible judgments the fearful part of you has.

To dig in a little deeper and get intimate with your fear, it can be helpful to look at your fear under the microscope to understand what it's really about.

Using one of the examples above, let's say you have a fitness goal and you tend to get lost in the comparison trap and that's where your resistance starts. Through curiosity you realize it ramps up and gets triggered around working out. You follow fitness influencers online and have noticed you compare yourself to them, feeling not good enough, not far along enough with your fitness goals, and you quit every few months or so.

A powerful inquiry to ask yourself here might be, *Why is this goal so important to me in the first place? Is it to feel healthy, look great to others, or something else?*

Getting intimate with your fear means taking the time to understand the patterns, triggers, and stories it feeds you—without judgment. By peeling back layers, you not only uncover what's really driving your resistance but also gain the clarity needed to challenge those stories. This process of curiosity and compassion is the foundation for breaking free and moving toward the life you truly want.

Step 3: Surrender and Accept

Step 3 in having a fierce throwdown with fear isn't what you might think it is. It's not figuring out a way to get rid of it or even make it less potent. Step 3 is to surrender to it and accept it.

After my dad died, I realized the grief was like a tsunami pulling me into it and churning away. I began to understand that fighting it was not only futile but making things worse. After a short street fight with it—the outcome being me losing painfully—I surrendered.

My resistance was locked up in a couple of things: (1) my belief that I could outsmart my emotions—that I could somehow limit them into more manageable pieces that were easier for consumption; and (2) my emotions scared me, especially the big, intense ones such as grief.

By pushing back on your fear, whatever it is, you're giving in to its power. Whether you're afraid to start a new business venture, make and show off your art, or process your emotions, when you fight the fear, put off the tasks around it, and beat yourself up, your fear wins.

Fear isn't something to outsmart or avoid—it's something to face, feel, and surrender to. Resistance, procrastination, and negative self-talk are just fear's clever disguises, keeping us stuck in a cycle of comfort and safety. By getting curious about your fear, uncovering its stories, and choosing to rewrite them, you can stop wrestling with it and start moving forward. The magic happens when you let fear walk alongside you while you take brave, unapologetic steps toward the life you truly want.

5

Say What You Mean

Living like you give a damn includes creating strong connections with others. There is a direct correlation between our happiness and fulfillment and the health of our relationships, so there's no getting out of this one. If you give a damn about your life and going after your goals, putting effort into your relationships is mandatory. Although it can be complicated at times, the payoff will be worth it.

We all want the same thing: to get what we want. But in terms of our communication, how we get there can seem like we're off-roading on a boulder-filled trail, driving a 1977 Volkswagen Bug with ten people piled in. Bumpy, uncomfortable, and the hard way.

There are several methods of terrible communication—for example, being passive-aggressive or sarcastic, hinting or even being manipulative to try to convey what you want, not saying what you want in hopes that other people read your mind, or waiting too long to ask for what you want.

Where You Might Be Getting It Wrong

If you've listed "Fluent in English, Spanish, and sarcasm" on your résumé, let's chat. There are various kinds of poor communication, and sarcasm is just one—but it's a common one.

Of course, it's fine to use sarcasm within your sense of humor now and then, but when you're using it to avoid, deflect, or even hurt someone else, there's a problem.

Being passive-aggressive is another poor communication style (and my bad communication style of choice, to be honest). Passive-aggression is the act of indirectly expressing your feelings—usually difficult ones like anger, frustration, or hurt—rather than being open about them. Passive-aggression can look like shifting blame, patronizing, weaponized kindness, denying anger, and fake politeness and innocence. Maybe you're thinking about people in your life who do this (maybe yourself?). Passive-aggression happens commonly within families and intimate relationships, and is also prevalent in the workplace.

On the far end of the ill-communication spectrum is using manipulation to try to get what you want. This is never okay. Using manipulation chronically is a surefire way to deteriorate relationships. So, please, don't be that asshole.

John M. Gottman, author of many books on relationships including *The Seven Principles for Making Marriage Work*, has built his career on, among many things, studying communication between romantic couples—specifically what kinds of communication are sure to create problems and ultimately end a relationship. According to Gottman, some of the most destructive forms of communication contain contempt and criticism. Contempt looks like eye-rolling, making someone feel like you're better than them, or making it clear you think they're stupid. Criticism is similar—mostly putting someone or their behavior down.

Bad communication styles aside, let's talk about why you sometimes (or often) have less than stellar communication. Maybe it's because you simply feel like being a jackass because someone hurt you, which happens. But my bet is that your poor communication stems from a fear that the other person can't or won't give you what you want or need. When you assume you're not going to get what you want, it becomes easier to have poor communication or salsa dance around the topic rather than to ask for what you want and possibly be disappointed by someone. Consequently, it becomes habitual; even if you're aware you do this and want to do better, you lack the skills to do so and never do. So, the cycle continues.

Sometimes we fall into bad communication because we're impatient and we want what we want. Sometimes it's just part of our personality. (Or maybe you blame your zodiac sign. As an Aries, I admit my delivery can come with a firebomb.) It may be because you just don't know how to communicate effectively. No matter the reason, we get to a certain age and it's our responsibility to fix how we express ourselves.

That time is now.

Before we dig further into this topic, allow me to let you off the hook for a moment and say that, most likely, no one taught you effective and healthy communication. If communication is something you struggle with, it's likely because you were raised by flawed humans who were also raised by flawed humans. Therefore it's reasonable to assume none of them knew how to deliver a difficult conversation with love and clarity. Instead they relied on stumbling awkwardness, raised voices, and vague demands.

Rare is the person who grows up learning how to do it right. So, unless you've sought out ways to communicate like a champ, you probably have some learning to do like the rest of us animals.

To your credit, many people adopt ill ways of communicating not only because it was modeled for them growing up but also because of past trauma or stress in the moment. If this is you, again, I urge you to do your best not to beat yourself up for it. One of the great things about being human is that, with some effort, we can change behavior we don't like.

What Happens If You Don't Say What You Mean?

Allow me to be the most forward and frank that I can be. If this is you, if you are someone who uses sarcasm, passive-aggression, denial of anger, or even manipulation when you communicate: Stop lying. It might sound harsh, but having terrible ways of communicating is essentially like lying. You're not being truthful about what it is you're trying to express. So, stop lying to the other person about what you want or don't want. Stop lying to yourself that there's no way you can get what you want or that your wants and needs don't matter. Stop lying that proper and healthy communication is too hard and that you don't know where to start.

When you regularly use poor communication, you are very rarely, if ever, going to get what you truly want. Using it long term is a surefire way to deteriorate relationships. It builds resentment in all parties involved, and resentment breeds anger, shame, and sometimes thoughts of revenge.

When you say what you mean, you're being true to yourself and leaning into your genuine ideals—the things and ways of living that are important to you. When you say what you mean, you're being courageous, respecting others, and loving the hell out of yourself.

So, let's talk about how to say what you mean. Where to even begin? The only place to start has nothing to do with having to talk with anyone. Rather, it's to first accept and understand that a new way of communicating is going to be uncomfortable—sometimes extraordinarily uncomfortable. It will require vulnerability, sitting through awkward conversations and silences, and a tremendous amount of courage from you. My hope is that you accept this mission. If so, let's begin.

How to Say What You Mean

What happens if you're a chronic sarcasm user, perhaps as recent as this morning, and you want to redeem yourself? What if after reading this chapter, you realize you are passive-aggressive to your partner or someone else in your life and you want to change? It's not too late to clean it up. I invite you to return to the person and say something like, "Hey, this morning I was sarcastic/passive-aggressive about X, and I shouldn't have been. That's unfair of me to not be clear about what I want, and I want to first apologize for communicating that way. So, here is what I'm really feeling . . ." And you go from there.

Yes, it's risky. Yes, the other person might not respond the way you want. Yes, this may make you so nervous you'll be running to the bathroom praying there's enough toilet paper for what's unfortunately about to happen. And yes, this is a step in the right direction of your relationship with this other person—whether it's a partner, coworker, or friend. It is more likely to yield positive results than running around in circles, not getting what you want, then throwing your hands in the air, feeling pissed off and resentful that they aren't hearing you and giving you what you need.

You have two choices, and you know what they are. One is easy and what you're used to; the other is hard and will require you to try something new and be brave. The latter is the one that will, in the long run, make you feel good about who you see in the mirror—and that, my friend, is why you picked up this book.

Hard Conversations

Saying what you mean is also about learning how to set boundaries and have hard conversations. These two things are some of the hardest skills of adulting. You'd probably rather sit next to someone on a plane eating a hot tuna sandwich (and you have the middle seat), but boundaries and hard conversations are as necessary as learning how to manage your money, apologize sincerely, and fold a fitted sheet (although that last one is debatable).

Be kind and clear in your communication. If it's a big deal, prepare ahead of time, just like you would for a job interview or when you're meeting your partner's parents for the first time. (Yes, it will likely feel awkward to practice "Hi, it's so nice to meet you, what a lovely home you have" in the bathroom mirror.) Act and behave as if you care about the conversation, because if you didn't care, you wouldn't feel the need to have the talk in the first place. You're obviously invested in the relationship, and investments require care. Don't be the kind of person who invests more time and care into their houseplants than their communication with people they care about. Even if the other person isn't offering the same kind of investment by getting better with their communication, it's still up to you to make the first move. Be the leader here and learn how to have better correspondence, even if it ends up being a one-way street in that regard. Sometimes being the example will eventually (not always) get others to follow your lead. Even if they don't, you've shown up as the best version of yourself.

GETTING TO WORK WITH HARD CONVERSATIONS

In an effort to prepare, get out a sheet of paper and answer the following questions:

- **Is this the type of relationship or situation where you can start with gratitude?** For example, "I love that you make me feel comfortable enough where I can come to you about hard things, and I have something I need to say..." Gratitude has the tendency to diffuse a tense situation and sets the stage for an open conversation.

- **Is this the type of situation where you need to acknowledge something first?** For instance, "I want to start by saying that many times my communication skills aren't the best, and it's something I'm actively working on. I also want to say that when you said X the other day, here's how it made me feel . . ." You're taking responsibility that you might have done the very thing you're about to ask them to change, which shows you're truly reciprocating responsibility for the relationship, whether it's romantic or not.

- **What is it that you want?** Before you have the conversation, get clear on what it is that you are hoping to get. Do you just want the other person to hear you? Do you want them to change something about their behavior? Do you want an apology? Once you're clear on this, remember to express whatever it is you want with kindness and clarity about what it is you're asking for. But remember: You have no control over how they'll respond to this or whether you'll get what you want.

- **What will constitute a win for you?** I'm emphasizing with great passion and ferocity that the win here—your utmost success and what makes you a badass in this situation—is not tethered to whether you get what you want but that you showed up with courage, tried something new, and made yourself proud. You can't control the outcome, how that person will experience your words, or how they'll react. The success rests squarely on if and how you show up.

Remember: There is a parallel between the health, happiness, and fulfillment of your life and well-being of your relationships. Healthy communicating takes practice, getting it wrong, tweaking, and having more hard conversations that will ultimately lead to better communication. This isn't just a "Maybe I'll get around to it later" type of task. If you want your life to be better, saying what you mean and learning to communicate like your soul depends on it is critical. You're smart and resourceful, so put those attributes to work.

6

Learn to Parent Yourself

One of the things no one tells us when we hit that magical age of eighteen and are thrust into the wide and wild world of adulthood is this: We need to learn to be an adult and parent ourselves.

But... what does that even mean?

You're standing there with your high school diploma, maybe a vague plan for the future, and a whole lot of confusion. Suddenly you're expected to have it all figured out. Spoiler alert: Most of us don't. (If you're still out here occasionally having cereal for dinner, you're in good company.)

When it comes to our personal growth and evolution, we need to learn to take care of ourselves physically, financially, and spiritually. But also emotionally and mentally. The good news? Learning to parent (or "reparent") yourself is a lifelong journey—it's not some checkbox or final exam you can fail. And the even better news? You don't need to do it perfectly to get it right. Think of it like assembling IKEA furniture: You'll probably end up with a few leftover screws, but it's still going to work.

What Happens If You Don't Learn to Reparent Yourself?

So, what if we don't go down this path of learning to reparent ourselves? What's at stake if we skip this inner work and just keep moving forward without addressing those needs that didn't get met as kids or that we never learned? To put it bluntly: a lot. Not taking the time to reparent ourselves can keep us locked in unhelpful, self-sabotaging cycles that hold us back from the life we want to live. When we don't address and work through these foundational needs, the consequences can show up in different areas of our lives, often in sneaky ways that affect us on the daily. This can feel like a slow burn over time, or a punch square in the nose.

To begin, there's the pesky issue of repeating painful patterns. If we don't do the work to fill in the emotional gaps left by our early experiences, we tend to keep seeking out people, situations, and behaviors that echo those same unmet needs. We tend to be unconsciously drawn to what's familiar, even if that familiar isn't healthy or fulfilling. Maybe you find yourself repeatedly attracted to people who aren't supportive or relationships that feel unbalanced. Or perhaps you stay in jobs or friendships that leave you feeling small or unheard. This isn't just bad luck—it's often because the unresolved pain is still running the show in the background, pulling us back to what we know, each time, deep down, hoping for a different outcome than the one you received previously.

Unresolved pain also makes it hard to form and maintain healthy relationships. When we haven't done the work of reparenting ourselves, we can struggle with issues like trust, boundaries, and emotional regulation, all of which are essential for meaningful, lasting connections. Relationships may feel more unstable or leave you feeling anxious, disconnected, or overly dependent. That's because if you haven't built up those inner resources, you're more likely to look to others to meet emotional needs that only you can truly fulfill. When those needs aren't met in a healthy way, it's easy to feel resentful, disappointed, or even self-critical—kind of like when you text someone "I'm fine" and they don't immediately reply with "Are you sure? Let's unpack this." It's a tricky dance, expecting others to fill the gaps that only you can patch. And let's be honest—no one likes feeling like they're auditioning for the role of your therapist.

Then there's the impact on our self-worth and inner dialogue—also known as the inner-critic. When we don't reparent, it's easy to carry around a sense of inadequacy, a persistent feeling of "I'm not good enough," which can lead to self-sabotage or paralyzing self-doubt. You might notice your harsh inner critic shows up every time you try something new or feel a little vulnerable. This inner critic? Often it's just the voice of old wounds and unmet needs talking, keeping you stuck in a place of fear rather than growth. If left unchecked, that critical inner voice can be a major roadblock, making it difficult to take risks, set healthy goals, or believe you're worthy of love and success.

Lastly, unaddressed wounds can also hold us back from discovering and growing into our best, most authentic selves. If we're still operating from a place of unmet needs and unresolved pain, it's like wearing a pair of foggy glasses. We're seeing the world—and ourselves—through a lens of past hurt, which can cloud our judgment and keep us from exploring new paths, meeting new people, and expressing our unique strengths and passions. When we reparent ourselves, we clear away that fog, allowing us to see the world and our place in it more clearly. But without it, we risk living a life that's more about survival than self-fulfillment, limiting our potential and the joy we're capable of experiencing.

In short, skipping the process of reparenting means carrying forward unresolved pain that shapes our choices, our relationships, and even our self-image. But by choosing to reparent ourselves, we get to break these patterns, build a stronger and healthier inner foundation, live life in a way that truly feels fulfilling and free, and live like you give a damn. (IKEA furniture assembly not required!)

How to Accept the Reality of Your Pain

Reparenting is a buzzword that's having a moment in the personal growth space. And for good reason! It can refer to a type of psychotherapy where the therapist takes on the role of a new or substitute parental figure for the client. This approach aims to address psychological issues resulting from inadequate or abusive parenting.

However, for self-help goals, you can work on reparenting on your own. I've broken this down into five categories of growth: recognizing what you missed; becoming the person you needed; setting boundaries; identifying, managing, and expressing emotions; and filling in the gaps.

First things first: Let's talk about accepting the reality of any pain or hurt you've experienced. This is a tough pill to swallow because it requires you to be truly honest with yourself and face some incredibly difficult circumstances and the feelings that surround them. Maybe you had a rough childhood, faced some serious challenges, or were let down by the people who were supposed to support you. I encourage you to do this reflection with a therapist or counselor because it will require you to acknowledge it, sit with that pain, and feel it. This isn't about wallowing in self-pity; it's about recognizing that your feelings matter. Your younger self will appreciate the acknowledgment, and the goal is to understand that those experiences have shaped you, for better or worse.

Here's an unpopular opinion: You do *not* need to forgive anyone in order to heal and move on. Forgiveness is often touted as the ultimate step to healing, but let's be real—sometimes we can't define forgiveness, or it's not possible, or it isn't necessary. Your healing is about you, not about absolving others of their wrongdoings. It's okay to carry some unresolved feelings as long as you're working through them in a healthy way.

Recognizing What You Missed

Now, let's move on to recognizing what you missed out on as a child, teenager, or young adult. This can be anything from emotional support to basic life skills. Take some time to reflect on your upbringing. What did you need that you didn't get? Maybe you needed more encouragement, more structure, or just consistency. Whatever it is, acknowledge it. This isn't about blaming your parents or caregivers; it's about understanding the gaps in your development so you can fill them yourself.

Becoming the Person You Needed

Next up, it's time to discover the kind of person you need to become—the person that child version of you needed and still needs. This exercise is one of my personal favorites because it can be incredibly empowering.

- **Envision the caregiver you needed.** Start by imagining the ideal caregiver for your younger self. Grab a piece of paper or open your favorite note-taking app. What qualities do they have? Are they patient, loving, and encouraging? Are they understanding, compassionate, and always supportive? Write these down. These are the traits that are important to you and that you're going to work on cultivating in yourself.
- **Write a letter to your younger self.** Be the person you needed to hear from back then. Offer words of comfort, support, and wisdom. Reassure your younger self that it's okay to feel what they're

feeling and that you've got their back now. This exercise is not only healing but also a powerful way to connect with your inner child.

Becoming the person you needed and need is about stepping into that role for yourself, not just in a one-time exercise but as an ongoing practice. You are no longer that child searching for someone to show up for them—you get to show up for yourself now. The more you practice this, the more it becomes second nature. And that, my friend, is where real healing happens.

Setting Boundaries

Let's talk about boundaries, both with yourself and others. Boundaries are essential for protecting your mental and emotional well-being. This starts by setting boundaries with yourself. It might look like working to shift your negative self-talk, prioritizing self-care, or making a commitment to pursue your goals and passions. Self-boundaries are about creating a safe space within yourself where you can thrive.

Next, set boundaries with others. This can be challenging, especially if you're used to people-pleasing or avoiding hard conversations at all costs. But remember, boundaries are a form of self-respect and wanting relationships to be stronger. They're about defining what is and isn't acceptable in your interactions with others. Be clear, be firm, and put energy and effort into enforcing your boundaries once they're set. You're not responsible for how others react to your boundaries; you're responsible for how you show up in them and for maintaining them.

Identifying, Managing, and Expressing Emotions

Buckle up, because here comes another challenging part. Learning to identify, manage, and express your emotions is another crucial part of reparenting. Many of us weren't taught how to deal with our emotions in a healthy way, so this is a major aspect that was left out. Maybe you were told to "Suck it up" or "Stop crying." Now's the time to unlearn those harmful messages.

Start by identifying your emotions. This might seem basic, but it's foundational. When you feel something, name it. (If this is challenging due to previous trauma, an inability to express or define your feelings, or other reasons, try working with a therapist.) Are you sad, angry, anxious, excited? Naming your emotions gives you power over them. Next, learn to manage your emotions. This doesn't mean suppressing them but rather finding healthy ways to cope and allowing the experience of the emotion to move through you. This could be through journaling, talking to a friend or therapist, exercising, or practicing mindfulness.

Lastly, express your emotions. This can be scary, especially if you're not used to being vulnerable. But expressing your emotions is a key part of emotional health. Share your feelings with trusted people in your life. Use "I" statements to communicate how you feel without placing blame. For example, "I feel hurt when..." or "I feel overwhelmed because..." This not only helps you process your emotions but also fosters deeper connections with others.

Filling in the Gaps

Finally, dig into anything else you need to learn what wasn't given or taught to you. This is your opportunity to become the most kick-ass version of yourself. Make a list of what to focus on monthly or yearly. Maybe you need to learn financial literacy, develop better communication skills, or cultivate a healthier relationship with food. Whatever it is, commit to learning and growing in those areas.

Self-parenting is about taking responsibility for your own development. It's about recognizing that while you can't change the past, you have the power to shape your future. It's about becoming the person you needed when you were younger and giving yourself the love, support, and guidance you deserve.

So, here's your invitation: Take this journey of self-parenting seriously. Embrace the challenges, celebrate the victories, and never stop growing. You're on your way to becoming the most kick-ass version of yourself, and I'm cheering you on every step of the way. Remember, you've got this. You're stronger, wiser, and more capable than you know. Now go out there and show the world what you're made of.

7

You Will Disappoint People

Years ago, I had a client, Lisa, who had always had a tricky relationship with her dad. She knew he loved her, but he had this way of completely disregarding her boundaries, as if they were optional or even offensive to him. When Lisa was growing up, her dad's presence was overbearing; he expected her to be available whenever he wanted, to share every detail of her life, and he'd even question her decisions if they didn't align with his views. Whenever Lisa tried to set a limit, he'd push back—hard. Sometimes he'd get hurt; other times, angry. She'd be left feeling guilty, as if she'd done something wrong just by speaking up for herself and being her own person, separate from him.

Over the years, instead of speaking to him directly about the problem, Lisa attempted to distance herself. She tried setting smaller boundaries, like cutting back on weekly calls and limiting how much she shared. But no matter how gently she tried to reinforce these boundaries, her dad bulldozed right through them. If she didn't answer a call, he'd text multiple times. If she didn't visit during the holidays, he'd guilt her for "abandoning" the family. Her mom would often call to smooth things over, urging her to "understand his feelings" or "just try to keep the peace." Her two younger sisters stood by, watching as Lisa carried the emotional weight of his demands.

When she finally reached out to me for coaching around what to do, she was drained. The cycle of guilt, anger, and exhaustion had left her feeling like a shell of herself. She resented her dad but couldn't imagine completely cutting off contact—it felt extreme, even selfish. She worried that going "no contact" even for a while would devastate her dad and send shock waves through the family. Her mom would be heartbroken, and she could already hear the whispers from her sisters, asking why she'd "hurt him like that." The thought of disappointing everyone made her stomach turn, and honestly, she half expected her family to draft an official breakup announcement for the Christmas letter—right next to the photo of the dog in a Santa hat.

Let's get real for a second. How many times have you felt like Lisa, when you held back, bit your tongue, or went along with something you didn't want to or truly believe in because you were afraid of disappointing someone? I know you've been there—I've been there. We all have. It's that gut-wrenching feeling that if we don't show up exactly as others expect us to, we're letting them down. And the kicker? This fear of disappointing others leaves us paralyzed, trapped in a loop of *What if they think less of me?* or *What if I'm not good enough?* But here's the harsh reality: When we fail to act because of that fear, we end up disappointing the one person who matters most. You guessed it—ourselves.

What Happens If You Consistently Choose to Disappoint Yourself?

Now, don't get me wrong. I know it's not as simple as just snapping your fingers and suddenly not caring what people think. We're wired to seek approval, connection, and belonging. It's a survival instinct. But here's the thing: We've taken this instinct and blown it out of proportion. We've allowed the opinions and expectations of others to dictate our actions, often at the expense of our own values and desires. And that, my friend, is where the real disappointment lies.

Let's unpack this a bit. Why do we care so damn much about what others think? Why does the idea of disappointing others feel like the end of the world? The answer is rooted in our need for connection. From a young age, we're taught to seek approval from those around us—our parents, teachers, friends. We learn that if we make others happy, we will be rewarded with love, attention, and acceptance. So naturally we start to equate approval with worthiness. If people like us, we must be doing something right. If they don't, well, there must be something wrong with us, right?

Here's the thing: Most of the time, it's not even about us. The expectations and standards we stress over are often projections of what other people think they need or want. We internalize these expectations and make them our own, twisting ourselves into knots trying to meet them. But these expectations are just that—expectations. They're not facts, and they're certainly not gospel. They're someone else's idea of how the world should be. They have nothing to do with who we are or our inherent worth.

So, let's work on flipping the script. Just for a moment, put aside worrying about how others perceive you. Then start asking yourself, *By doing [insert thing you're doing to not disappoint others], am I living in alignment with my own values? Am I being true to myself?* Because at the end of the day, *you* are the one who has to live with the choices you make. *You* are the one who has to look in the mirror and be okay with what you see. If you're consistently sacrificing your own needs, desires, and values to keep others happy, you're going to end up feeling pretty damn disappointed with yourself.

How to Stop Disappointing Yourself—It's Not Your Responsibility

Let's talk about responsibility. One of the biggest misconceptions we carry around is the belief that we're somehow responsible for other people's feelings. We think that if someone is upset, it's our fault. If they're disappointed, we've failed them. But let me be crystal clear here: *You are not responsible for how other people feel*—as long as you've conducted yourself with clarity, kindness, and in alignment with your values.

Look, I get it. We don't want to hurt people. We don't want to be the reason someone else feels pain or disappointment. But here's the truth: Other people's emotions are their own. You can't control how someone else reacts to your choices. You can only control how you show up in your conversations, with your energy, and in your relationships.

You've got to take care of *your* emotional well-being first. If you're constantly putting other people's needs, expectations, and feelings ahead of your own, you're going to run out of energy and patience pretty quickly, and resentment will set in.

EMPOWERMENT PRACTICE

This empowerment practice is about taking intentional steps toward actions that align with your values—even when they feel uncomfortable. It's a muscle you build over time, strengthening your confidence and autonomy so that you're less affected by others' reactions and more grounded in your own truth.

This practice is especially powerful when you know you have to do things that might disappoint others in order to stay true to yourself. And let's be real—that's going to happen. Some people are so easily offended that you could sneeze wrong and ruin their day. Your job? Not to take that on.

Step 1: Identify Where Discomfort Shows Up

Take a moment to reflect on where you feel resistance when it comes to prioritizing your own needs over others' expectations.

- Is there a decision you're delaying because you fear how someone will react?
- Are you hesitating to set a boundary or speak up about something important to you?
- Do you feel guilty when you say no, even when you know it's the right choice?

Write down one situation where you feel this tension. Simply naming it is the first step toward moving through it.

Step 2: Take a Small, Courageous Action

Start with something manageable—one small step toward prioritizing yourself. You might:

- Journal about the root of your fear—where it started, what you're truly afraid of, and what the best-case outcome might look like.
- Practice saying no to something minor and sitting with the discomfort, reminding yourself that you are not responsible for managing other people's emotions.
- Reframe a difficult action as an opportunity for growth instead of something to avoid.

Pick one and commit to doing it within the next forty-eight hours. No overthinking—just action.

Step 3: Expand Your Tolerance for Discomfort

As you get comfortable with small acts of courage, start applying this practice to bigger decisions. You might:

- Have that difficult conversation you've been avoiding.
- Set a firm boundary and stand by it, even if it makes someone uncomfortable.
- Take a risk on something that matters deeply to you, knowing that not everyone will approve.

The goal isn't to seek out conflict or upset people for sport (this isn't a reality-TV audition). The goal is to trust yourself enough to make decisions that serve you, even when they don't please everyone else.

Step 4: Reflect and Reinforce

After taking action, notice how you feel. Ask yourself:

- *What was the actual outcome versus the worst-case scenario I imagined?*
- *What did I learn about myself from this experience?*
- *How can I continue to build my tolerance for discomfort so I don't default to people-pleasing?*

The more you do this, the more you'll realize that disappointing others isn't the end of the world. In fact, it's often the beginning—the beginning of making decisions that honor you, feel authentic, and reinforce your self-trust.

Because living like you give a damn isn't about keeping everyone happy—it's about choosing yourself and knowing that you're worth it.

The Inevitable Choice: Disappoint Them or Disappoint Yourself

Here's the thing: There are going to be times when you have to make a choice. You're going to have to decide whether to disappoint someone else or disappoint yourself. As much as we'd all love to have our cake and eat it too, it's just not possible to please everyone all the time. The sooner you accept this, the freer you'll be.

When you choose to disappoint yourself in order to keep someone else happy, you're sending yourself a message: *Their needs are more important than mine. Their approval is worth more than my integrity.* Over time, that message chips away at your self-worth. It erodes your confidence and makes you feel like you're not enough. But when you choose to disappoint others in order to stay true to yourself, you're making a bold statement: *I am worthy of living a life that aligns with my values. My truth is more important than their expectations.*

And here's the beautiful part: When you start making choices that are true to who you are, you'll attract the right people into your life. The people who support your values and boundaries, and who respect you—they'll stick around. They'll appreciate the real you.

Choosing Yourself

So, here's where we land: Choose yourself. Every. Single. Time. Choosing yourself means choosing your well-being, values, and truth, especially when it's hard. Even when it means disappointing others. Even when it feels uncomfortable.

This doesn't mean turning into some kind of "Choose-Yourself Olympian," complete with a gold medal in boundary-setting (though that would be a pretty epic event). It just means learning to say no to the things that drain you and "Hell, yes" to the things that light you up—even if it ruffles a few feathers.

But here's what I promise you: As long as you do this with courage (and a side of discomfort), you will never disappoint yourself. You'll look back on your life and know that you lived it on your own terms. You'll know that you honored your own needs, desires, and values. And that, my friend, is the ultimate victory.

Getting back to Lisa. Through her work with me, Lisa got honest with herself. She unpacked the toll her dad's demands had taken on her mental health, relationships, and self-worth. I coached her around what she valued most—self-respect, inner peace, autonomy—and how these had consistently taken a back seat to keeping her dad happy. With support, she started envisioning what life might feel like with a real boundary in place, even if it meant a temporary break from her dad.

In one pivotal session, I asked Lisa to consider what advice she'd give to a friend in her shoes. The answer was clear as she blurted out, "I'd tell her to protect herself." Hearing those words out loud, Lisa felt a new resolve rise within her.

So, she did what she'd always been too scared to do. Lisa had a direct, calm conversation with her dad. She explained that she was going to step back for a bit and wouldn't be in touch for a while. As she expected, her dad reacted with anger, accusing her of being selfish and ungrateful. Her mom and other family members called too, urging her to reconsider, to think of how this was affecting everyone else. But Lisa held her ground. For the first time, she chose her own peace over their comfort.

It was painful, and there were moments she second-guessed herself. But in the silence, Lisa felt a profound sense of relief—a lightness she hadn't experienced in years. The guilt began to fade, replaced by a newfound respect for herself. Lisa knew she hadn't rejected her family; she'd simply chosen herself and was loving them temporarily from afar. As she navigated this new chapter, she realized that protecting her peace was a right, not something she had to apologize for. She was finally living life on her terms.

So, the next time you're faced with a choice between disappointing someone or disappointing yourself, I want you to ask yourself this: *If I choose them, am I betraying myself?* And if the answer is yes, then you know what you need to do. Choose you. Every time.

***

Remember, you are not responsible for other people's feelings. You are responsible for your own happiness, well-being, and truth. And that truth is worth more than all the approval in the world. So go out there and live it. Disappoint others if you must, but never, ever disappoint yourself.

8

Always Bet on and Choose Yourself

I, probably like you, have stayed in relationships far too long.

Past the time where I felt the tap on my shoulder, gently whispering that maybe it's time to think about walking away. Past the time where the pit in my stomach got deeper and wider. Past the time where my intuition then grabbed me by the shoulders and said clear as day, "Andrea, it's time to leave."

We stay in a relationship—whether it's a romantic partner, a job, a city, or anything else—because we're betting on the comfort. We're attached to the satisfaction we get from the familiar, even when the familiar has become uncomfortable.

We're also betting that it might get better, even if deep down we know that won't happen. Even if we push down and bury that knowledge that it won't happen. We cling to potential, we cling to crumbs, and we cling to the remote and minuscule possibility that things might improve.

We do this for many reasons—all of them drenched in fear. But the one I'll point out in this chapter is that often we don't leave relationships we know are over or make hard decisions where the action to be taken is risky because *we don't trust ourselves.*

We don't trust that we'll be okay alone. The thought of not having a partner can be too much to bear, and social conditioning tells us we're not a whole person unless we're partnered. We don't trust that we're making the right choice to leave. We make excuses for ourselves, our partners, our jobs, and our relationships. It's often easier to hold out hope that things will change (even if we know the truth is they won't) rather than take the risk of leaving.

We don't trust that we can find a different, even better job; that we can and will make friends if we move out of state; or that our life will in fact improve if we start, for once, putting ourselves first.

We don't trust that if we make the decision—even if we second-guess ourselves after it's done; even if we then determine that we've made the "wrong" decision—that we can figure out a way to make it "right," be okay, or course correct. We don't trust that we're inherently resilient.

We don't trust that our gut is telling us the truth. We're so used to bypassing it for the more "comfortable" way to try to solve the problem or ignoring it altogether.

Whether we're talking about trust or comfort zones, all of this comes down to vulnerability. It's vulnerable to trust ourselves, and vulnerability always equals risk. I am not here to write about a safety net and tell you if you jump, the net will appear, or even to trust a higher power bigger than yourself. That's amazing if you can do that, and I hope you do, but this is all about learning to trust the most important human that you'll always be faced with: yourself.

What Happens If You Don't Bet On and Choose Yourself?

We, as humans, are made up of different parts of ourselves. Sometimes we can even be categorized as hypocritical based on what we say we believe or what we say we'll do. For example, I've always had a propensity for risk, putting myself in situations where I'm surprised I made it out alive. My teenage kids are aghast at stories I tell them about my teenage years in the '90s. Getting in cars with strange boys, drinking Boone's Farm Strawberry Hill wine straight from the bottle at a field party with only the light from burning cigarettes or approaching headlights. Sneaking out my bedroom window on the second floor in the middle of the night without my parents having any way to track me or get a hold of me. And I was never afraid.

However, asking me to take a risk and bet on myself is another, more terrifying story. To have unwavering faith that I would have been okay leaving a long relationship that I knew was past its expiration date? To speak up for myself at my first corporate job and ask to negotiate my salary when I knew I was being underpaid? To move out on my own to a nearby area that I dreamed of living in, even though my boyfriend wouldn't move with me?

I would do none of those things.

And I'm guessing you may have a hard time taking risks on yourself as well. Maybe it's only about certain things or areas of your life, but it's still there.

The obvious consequence of not betting on ourselves is that we rarely get what we want when we don't. You may have heard the saying, "If you never ask, the answer will always be no." In other words, when we don't make that leap and take that risk, we stay where we are. The days become years, and before we know it, we're staring middle age in the crow's-feet-lined face, wondering how we got here so fast and a little panicked that our life isn't turning out how we wanted it to.

The other harsh reality is that most people aren't actually thinking about us as much as we might think they are. The Universe does not in fact revolve around us, so we have to—and I mean *have to*—work on trusting ourselves. In order to live this life like we give a damn, and to get what we want, we must take risks and bet on ourselves day after day, year after year.

How to Bet On and Choose Yourself

Getting clear on what you want isn't always easy—especially if you've spent years putting others first. So instead of asking *What do I want?* let's start with *What am I done tolerating?* Clarity begins by naming what no longer serves you. From there, it's about taking responsibility for your own happiness—because no one is coming to save you. And that's not a bad thing. It means *you* have the power to create the life you want.

Let's dive in.

Step 1 on Getting Clear

Let's start from the beginning. I will not ask you what you want. After many years of working with people on what they want more of in their lives, I can't tell you how many times I've asked women this and been met with a blank stare. Please know this is a common response, especially for a group of people who have traditionally put other people before themselves.

So, I'll start by asking you:

- What do you want less of in your life?
- What do you want to stop doing or accepting?
- What would you like to not have to worry about anymore?

Get out a piece of paper or your favorite note-taking app and write down your answers.

When engaging in this exercise, I invite you to be more honest than you think you should. Write it down and throw it away afterward, or password protect it on your phone. You may end up with answers like

> *I want to not be in this relationship anymore.*
> *I want to stop being the one who does everything and watches everyone sit around and expect me to do it all.*
> *I want to not have to worry about finances and also not hate my job.*
> *I want to not be triggered as an adult because of things that happened in my past.*

That should tell you what you want because it's usually some form of the opposite of what you don't want. If we're using the examples above, your list would probably look like this:

> *I want to know what needs to happen in order for me to leave this relationship.*
> *I want to have equality when it comes to running this household and to feel like I'm supported.*
> *I want to figure out my finances better and look for a job that I enjoy.*
> *I want to find a therapist I trust so that I can work on these issues that keep triggering me in relationships.*

In terms of getting clear on what you want, sometimes it can be helpful to look beyond what the "thing" is that you want and look at the feeling or experience you think you'll get once you have it.

If you want to leave a relationship, you probably hope to gain freedom and follow your instincts.

If you want support in the operations and/or physical labor in your household, you probably want to feel appreciated, valued, and like a team player.

If it's about finances, you might want to feel safe and secure.

It can be helpful to know this because there might be a way for you to get these feelings and experiences in other places as well as the things you're clear on that you want.

How you feel in your life matters just as much as the goals you have.

Understanding what you want often starts with clarity about what you don't want. By giving yourself permission to name the things you're done tolerating, you've taken an important step toward reconnecting with your needs and desires. And by looking beyond the surface to the feelings and experiences you're seeking, you've started to uncover what truly matters to you.

Step 2 on Getting Clear

The next step is to look at any places you need to take responsibility for. I know, you might have expected us to move straight away into how to get what you want, because after all, at this point you are someone who gives a damn about the way you live your life. However, when learning how to bet on yourself every time, we need to get to the place of understanding that when you bet on yourself, you are also accepting that no one is coming to save you.

Realistically, No One Is Coming to Save You

It's you. You are your own hero. You are your own hype girl. You are your own savior. (To be clear, yes, partners and friends and jobs should be in your life to support you. Emphasis on support. But you—you are in your life to always save yourself.)

So, in the past, have you consciously or unconsciously expected a partner to make you happy? Have you expected a job to pay your bills and be satisfying? Have you expected someone else to show up for your mental and emotional needs exactly as you needed to be supported and exactly when you needed to be supported? It's okay if you have—most of us do at some point. (Heck, I once spent three months thinking the right planner would turn me into Martha Stewart-level organized. Spoiler: It didn't.) Don't beat yourself up if you have had these expectations; that part is normal. But now is the time to realize where you've not only expected these things to make you happy but also where you've bet on these things to make you happy. If you've ever trusted that someone other than you will fulfill you and they've disappointed you, it's time to first give yourself grace for doing so, then check your expectations in the future.

THREE MAIN AREAS OF BETTING ON YOURSELF

Boundaries are hands down one of the hardest lessons I teach in my work, for my clients and community as well as for myself. Who knew that saying yes when you want to say yes and no when you want to say no could be so hard? Yet here we are.

Generations of social conditioning, the human experience of massive discomfort during hard conversations, and patterns of behavior have created generations of women who tend to struggle here. I say all of this in hopes that you give yourself enormous amounts of grace.

Have Good Boundaries

First, get clear on what's okay and what's not okay with the following:

- If you struggle with any relationship in your life, make a list of these struggles.

- After that, start pausing before you respond to requests, especially if it's one where you immediately know you want to answer in a way that might be hard for the other person to hear. *Betting on yourself requires you to know and believe that you will be okay no matter what the outcome is.*

Take Inventory of Your Self-Doubts and Address Them

To bet on yourself does not mean you're void of having any self-doubts. The vast majority of people have them at least at varying times in their lives (and the ones that don't, I'm not sure I believe them). Cut yourself some slack here—you're a normal human having a normal human existence.

Betting on yourself means that you look at the places where you doubt yourself. The places we doubt ourselves deserve to be in the spotlight and to be worked on. If you're asking, "Where do I even start?":

- Look at the places you doubt yourself. Get specific here.
- Get curious about what you uncovered in the previous bullet point. Ask yourself questions like, *Where did that likely come from?*
- Where do you lack confidence? Is it in your overall abilities, speaking up for yourself, or are you being hard on yourself for not "living up to your potential"?

When you dig in, get curious, and unpack what you find, you're essentially betting on your ability to grow in these places, even if it's a long, slow process (which, newsflash, it will be).

Trust Your Instincts

As I write this book, I'm about to turn fifty years old. If I had to tell my younger self just one thing, or if I had to leave my children—especially my daughter—with one piece of wisdom, and if I could only give you one bit of advice, it's this: Trust your gut, your instincts, your inner wisdom.

I've written several books, and in every single one I mention this. When you listen to your built-in instincts, you are betting on yourself. You're honoring ancient wisdom that is part of your DNA, part of your energy, and something unexplainable that is bigger than us. Our instincts help keep us alive, but not only that. They help us thrive. By trusting your instincts, you are showing up for yourself over and over again instead of walking away from yourself. To strengthen and trust your instincts:

- **Pause and check in with your body.** Your gut often speaks through physical sensations. Pay attention to what feels expansive (yes) or constricting (no).
- **Stop overriding your first reaction.** If something feels off, trust that feeling instead of talking yourself out of it.
- **Look at your past choices.** When you followed your instincts, how did it turn out? When you ignored them, what happened? Learn from your own history.
- **Practice on small things first.** Trust yourself in everyday decisions—what to eat, what to wear, whether to say yes or no—so it becomes second nature for bigger choices.
- **Release the need for outside approval.** Seeking validation weakens your inner voice. Trust yourself first, and let that be enough.

Trusting yourself isn't just about making better decisions—it's about honoring who you are, again and again, until it becomes second nature.

***

Betting on yourself is one of the most profound acts of self-trust and self-respect you can cultivate. It means stepping out of the illusion of comfort and facing the discomfort of growth, risk, and vulnerability. By exploring what you want less of, understanding the feelings behind what you truly desire, and taking responsibility for your life, you're laying the groundwork for real, meaningful change. It's not about perfection or fearlessness but rather learning to trust yourself enough to make bold choices, hold boundaries, and lean into your instincts. This is how you begin to create a life where you live like you give a damn.

9

Keep Your Side of the Street Clean

In my many decades here on earth, I've had lots of relationships—as I'm sure you have too—both romantic and mostly platonic. I've gotten some wrong and others right, and I can tell you there's a handful of things that are imperative in terms of creating peace and harmony in life that are in direct correlation to your relationships.

One of those things is learning how to "keep your side of the street clean."

Allow me to paint you a picture. You go into work, or you wake up in the morning at home, and someone has left you a mess. Perhaps the mess maker assumes you'll clean it up, or that you won't. Either way, you are upset that you have to look at it, and you try to work around the mess.

You're frustrated as well as angry and feel justified in your feelings. You might hold a grudge against this person, give them a piece of your mind or the silent treatment.

It's hard to not focus on this mess, isn't it? The audacity of them to make this disarray that impacts us, seemingly without any plans to clean it up. It would likely be challenging to focus on just this mess and not the person who made it.

Since we're all adults here, we can admit that sometimes we make these messes too. Sometimes we leave a mess out for others to see, and sometimes we shove everything into a closet, not really cleaning it up but hoping "out of sight, out of mind" will work.

In this metaphor, the mess can mean many things: bad behavior—someone else's or our own; poor communication; lying; hurting feelings; really anything that causes a negative reaction or consequence. A person's shortcomings or flaws that contributed to the mess can be real or perceived.

Keeping your side of the street clean means owning up and taking responsibility for your bad choices or behavior, cleaning up any "messes" that you make, and learning and moving on with better choices or behavior. It also includes working on letting go of focusing on the other side of the street—you're not responsible for anyone's behavior but your own.

What Happens If You Don't Keep Your Side of the Street Clean?

Although it may not seem like it, if left to our own devices, we would pretty much plow through life without a whole lot of regard for others. I'm not saying you or anyone else is an asshole (maybe, but probably not), but we generally don't grow up learning important things like taking true responsibility for our mistakes, not taking things personally, and only focusing on what *we* can do to improve ourselves or a situation.

When we don't focus on only keeping our side of the street clean, here are two possible consequences.

First, when we focus on others' behavior and shortcomings, we are essentially throwing someone else's trash all over our side. When this happens, we are distracted from our own world by their garbage, and it becomes easy to ignore things that need our attention in our life. Not to mention, we have little to no control over someone else's trash that we've allowed on our side, so it just sits there, festering and making us mad and frustrated.

For example, let's say you have a coworker who consistently misses deadlines, and their work impacts your own. You've pointed it out to them, maybe even to your boss, but nothing changes. Instead of focusing on how to adapt your workflow or manage your boundaries, you become hyperfixated on their behavior. You complain about it endlessly—probably to anyone within earshot—replaying scenarios in your head like it's a Netflix drama and losing hours of productivity stewing over their incompetence.

Here's the kicker: While you're over there mentally drafting a Ted Talk titled "Why My Coworker Sucks," your own deadlines start slipping. Or maybe your frustration spills over, and now you're snapping at people who didn't even do anything wrong (like Brenda in accounting—poor Brenda). Their mess? It's now all over your side of the street, not because they hauled it over with a wheelbarrow but because *you let it*. You've spent so much time griping about their trash that you've ignored your own.

Here's the truth you might not want to hear: You're not going to change them. You're not going to guilt them, inspire them, or annoy them into suddenly becoming a responsible human. The only thing you can change is how you think about it, your emotions about it, and how you handle it, whether that's getting clear on what you can control, putting up boundaries, or deciding to mentally drop-kick their mess right back to their side.

The other consequence is when we don't clean up our side of the street, we miss opportunities to develop and nurture relationships. When we don't deal with our own shit, we aren't growing, period. Plus, cleaning up messes, making amends where needed, and having the hard conversations that are necessary when we're making things right will build trust and nurture the relationship. It's vulnerable to take responsibility for mistakes we've made, and vulnerability in relationships often leads to more closeness and connection.

How to Keep Your Side of the Street Clean

Allow me to introduce to you the street sweepers. These are regular practices to do that will help keep your side of the street clean. (I want to pause to say, if you're like me—someone who feels much more comfortable complaining about my dirty street and throwing the trash back on others—I feel you. But please trust me when I say street sweeping is really the best way to live like you give a damn.)

Bear with me as we run with this metaphor and beat it to death, in the nicest of ways. Let's look at some of the "cleanup tools" you can employ to focus on keeping your side of the street clean. Because ultimately it's about tending to the street.

Releasing the Illusion of Control

Step 1: Get out a piece of paper or your favorite note-taking app and, if you can, draw two lines down the page to create three columns. In the first column, make a list of all the people who've wronged you, whether it was ten years ago or more, or just this week. No need to go into great detail about it for now; just their name and a brief synopsis of the trash they left on your street.

Step 2: In the middle column, list on a scale of 0 to 5 how much control you have or had over changing that situation (0 being none, 5 being all the control). If it's a low number (which it likely is), jot down two things: First, how it's affecting you to keep holding out hope that you can change the situation. Second, how it's affecting you to hope that the other person will do what you'd like them to do.

Step 3: In the last column, write out how your life would improve if you could let that go. If you can realistically let that person deal with their own trash, even if that trash irritates you, makes you mad and want to throw things... like knives. Feel free to also add what action you can take to try to solve the problem (that only you can do) and if you can remain unattached to if they'll clean up their trash.

Here's an example:

Parents didn't show up for me emotionally like I needed them to when I was growing up.	0 (no control over the way they parented), and it's negatively affecting me to keep holding out hope or thinking I can change the past.	My life would improve if I dealt with the hurt I have from not getting what I needed and allowed the experience to be what it is instead of being attached to wishing things were different.
Partner forgot our anniversary.	1 or 2 (no control over partner's memory, but I could have reminded them). It's negatively affecting me to think I can change the situation, and it's making me ruminate on when they'll start remembering things like this.	My life would improve and I'd feel better if I talked to my partner about putting reminders in their phone about important dates like this and emphasized how these types of things make me feel loved. And then let them take responsibility.

This exercise should help you see the ways it's mostly negatively impacting *you* by holding on to the fantasy that you can change things on your own. Focusing on their trash or trying to clean it up is not for you to do.

This isn't about letting people off the hook for things you need. You still are entitled to communicate things like hurt, disappointment, or your needs. You are also entitled to feel however you feel about each scenario. Instead, this is about *after* you communicate what you need, allowing the other person to own what they're responsible for. Then you are only in charge of your side of the street—how you think and behave from there on out.

Practicing Mindful Cleanup

Another "street sweeper" is mindfulness. I like to define mindfulness as paying attention or self-awareness because "mindfulness" can sound very serious, heavy, and like we need to be present at every single moment. (You don't. Simply practice paying attention.)

When we're not paying attention, we let people throw trash wherever they want, and we leave it there to fester and stink. After a while we can't figure out where that "smell" is coming from—more specifically, why we're mad or disappointed. For instance, if you walk away from interactions with certain people and don't feel great afterward, think about what the interaction entailed. Was it riddled with disparaging gossip about someone, and although it felt fun and like a moment of bonding, when you're done, you felt a little gross? Maybe next time change the subject when the gossip becomes defamatory. If the other person wishes to converse in that way, that can be their business, but they don't need to bring it to you.

Slowing Down to Gain Clarity

Yoga, meditation, and things like walking in nature (or even in the city) are ways to slow down your mind and thus practice mindfulness. By doing this, you're more likely to gain awareness and get clarity on specific instances where you might need to work on letting go or shifting to focus on your side of the street.

Journaling is another way to slow down and get clear. Journaling tends to be one of those exercises people cast aside because they don't see an immediate return on investment, they're not sure they're "doing it right," or they feel stuck about what to write.

There is no wrong or right way to journal. Most of my journaling is one or two sentences, and that's just to keep me in the habit of the exercise. When the time comes and I have more to scribble down, I do that.

Exploring Mindfulness Through Learning

Reading or listening to books on spirituality is another powerful way to cultivate mindfulness. The topic doesn't have to be heavy or overly academic—find something that resonates with you and meets you where you're at. Maybe it's a book that helps you reflect on your values or inspires you to think differently about your relationships and experiences. Even if it's just a five-minute audiobook session while folding laundry, create little moments where you can pause, reflect, and get curious about what's showing up in your life.

Identifying and Patching Your Potholes

If we're really going to bring it on home with this clean-street metaphor, also look for the "potholes" on your street—the things that might not seem like a big deal at first but can cause damage if left unchecked. These could be certain people you have a hard time setting or keeping boundaries with. Maybe you feel yourself giving in to their demands or letting their behavior throw you off course. That's a pothole. It might also look like not getting enough sleep, where every late night chips away at your energy and leaves you snapping at people the next day. Or perhaps it's a particular hot topic that instantly sets you off—politics at the dinner table, that coworker's tone in meetings, or conversations that dredge up old wounds.

Potholes are sneaky. They can make you stumble or throw you completely off-balance, especially when you don't see them coming. But once you know where they are, you can avoid them—or better yet, patch them up. Awareness is key. Pay attention to what consistently trips you up and take steps to smooth it out. After all, the fewer potholes on your street, the smoother your ride.

***

Here's the thing: Your street, your life, is yours. When you tend to it with care—owning your messes, letting go of the things you can't control, and paying attention to what's really going on—you create an environment that's not just livable but thriving. Sure, people will still toss trash, potholes will still pop up, and parked cars might block your way, but with the tools you've got, you'll know how to handle them. You don't have to fix the whole neighborhood; you just have to keep your corner clean. That's where the magic happens. That's where peace, growth, and connection live. Keep sweeping, my friend. You're worth it.

10

How You Do One Thing Is Not How You Do Everything

In my years of working in the personal development space, I've heard every motivational quote under the sun. It's like we've got a collection of go-to phrases we pull out when we need a quick boost—or, let's be real, when we don't know what else to say to someone who needs a pep talk. The problem is, a lot of these sound bite-size pieces of advice oversimplify personal growth, turning them into things we can slap on a meme or drop in a podcast sign-off.

One of the most common and frankly problematic sayings I hear is "How you do one thing is how you do everything." It's plastered everywhere—on motivational posters, spoken by bosses, and preached by fitness professionals. While there are plenty of quotes I could call out here, this one stands out because it sets us up for failure with its binary thinking. It's a classic example of what psychologists call *dichotomous thinking*, which is all about seeing life in terms of black or white, right or wrong, good or bad. And I see it often in my community.

It's easy to fall for this way of thinking. It's simple, it's clean, and let's face it—it offers a false sense of control in a world that feels unpredictable and messy. But here's the kicker: That simplicity is a trap. This all-or-nothing mindset overlooks the beautiful messiness of life. We forget that humans are complex creatures and life is filled with nuance. The pressure to live with such a rigid perspective can lead to burnout and a whole lot of self-criticism. Worst of all, it takes away our ability to have compassion—both for ourselves and others. It's time we start embracing the messy middle and reject the idea that everything needs to be "perfect" to be valuable.

What Happens If You Think in Terms of Black or White?

If you are a dichotomous thinker, ride or die, the impact will be far-reaching and likely to wreak havoc in several areas of your life. First off, this type of binary thinking can sabotage your relationships. When you see everything as black or white, you're more likely to categorize people as either allies or enemies, good or bad. This makes it nearly impossible to see the nuances in others—their complexity, their contradictions, their growth. As a result, you lose the ability to empathize, communicate openly, or collaborate effectively, and misunderstandings start to pile up. Eventually those little rifts turn into bigger issues, driving wedges between you and those you care about.

But it doesn't stop there. On a broader scale, black-and-white thinking contributes to the polarization and division that's become so prevalent in our society. It feeds into extremism, intolerance, and a refusal to engage in real, meaningful dialogue. Instead of seeking common ground or understanding, the world becomes divided into dehumanization and an us-versus-them mentality—no space for the middle ground, no room for nuance or growth.

This mindset not only keeps us stuck in our personal lives but also isolates us from the potential to grow together as a society. By clinging to these oversimplified views, you miss out on the richness of human connection, the depth of personal transformation, and the opportunity to create a more compassionate and collaborative world. You'll find yourself constantly frustrated and exhausted from trying to live up to an impossible standard, and your relationships and communities will suffer for it.

How to Change Dichotomous Thinking

Let's talk about how to shift away from black-and-white thinking. If we want to do this, the first step is self-awareness. Yup, it's a fancy way of saying, "Pay attention to what you're doing." We can't solve a problem if we don't know what it looks like and how to recognize it when it's happening. It's essential to start by seeing quickly and clearly when you're slipping into the trap of binary thinking. Because as you already know, life is rarely as simple as "right or wrong" or "good or bad." It's more like a cocktail of both, with a twist of growth, learning, and "Oh shit, I didn't see that coming." So, the next time you find yourself jumping to extremes—like, *I'm either winning at life or I'm a complete failure*—pause and ask, *Is this really the full picture? Are there shades of gray I'm missing?* Trust me, there are. Developing awareness is the first step in shifting your mindset because without it, you're like a hamster on a wheel going nowhere.

Quitting Like a Winner

Now let's talk about quitting for one hot second. I know, I know. Quitting often gets a bad rap. We've been brainwashed into thinking that walking away from a goal means we've failed or that we're somehow not good enough. But here's the truth: Quitting doesn't make you a failure; it makes you a boundary-setting, self-respecting human. Seriously. If you change your mind about your goals, that's perfectly okay. Maybe your original goals were more about impressing someone else than about what you actually want. Maybe you're halfway through and realize you'd rather be taking a nap with your dog and not stressing over it. No shame in that!

But quitting because you think productivity equates to your worth, or you're terrified of failing, or you think people will judge you—that's when you're quitting for the wrong reasons. Your goals, your dreams, your voice—they matter. And for the love of everything holy, your truth matters. If you're walking away from something because it no longer serves you or you realize you're doing it for someone else, that's not failure. That's evolution. It's growth. It's you choosing yourself, and that's always the right decision. So, repeat after me: "I'm not doing life wrong." You're letting yourself change and evolve, which is pretty much the opposite of wrong.

Practicing Self-Compassion and Shifting Your Thinking

It's time to show yourself some kindness. If you've been beating yourself up over past decisions—like not finishing college or whatever other unfinished business is still haunting you—it's time to cut yourself some slack. You're giving way too much power to what you perceive as "mistakes," and that's where you're getting stuck. You can love yourself and be compassionate with yourself—even if you "quit" something. Every decision you've made up until now has brought you here. And guess what? You've learned from those decisions. You've grown. You are worthy of all the love and grace you can throw at yourself.

Now that we've addressed quitting, let's talk about shifting your thinking. To truly break free from black-and-white thinking, you need to practice self-compassion and acceptance. It's time to acknowledge that making mistakes or facing challenges doesn't mean you're a failure—it means you're human. It may sound obvious and even cheesy, but it's imperative that you acknowledge this. In fact, it's often in the gray areas where we confront our vulnerabilities and true growth happens. Life is not about having all the answers or always being "right." It's about learning from every experience, whether that experience is labeled a success or a setback. Embrace the process—because that's where resilience and badassery happen.

- **Step 1: Notice where you're being hard on yourself.** Think about the decisions or situations you keep replaying in your mind. The things that still haunt you, the regrets that won't seem to loosen their grip. What are you holding over your own head? Take a moment to acknowledge them without judgment.
- **Step 2: Reframe what you see as "mistakes."** Instead of letting these moments define you, look at what they've taught you. What have you learned? How have you grown? Every single decision you've made has led you here, and nothing is wasted if you gained something from it—even if it's just the realization of what you *don't* want.
- **Step 3: Give yourself some damn grace.** It's time to practice self-compassion. That means shutting down the voice in your head that tells you you're not enough. It means recognizing that life is messy, and evolving is part of the deal. Maybe that looks like journaling a few sentences about how far you've come or simply reminding yourself that you are allowed to change, grow, and rewrite your story.

This isn't about toxic positivity or pretending things didn't hurt. It's about allowing yourself to move forward without dragging past decisions around like dead weight. The more you practice this, the more you'll see that resilience isn't about getting everything right—it's about learning, adjusting, and giving yourself the love and grace you deserve.

Expanding Your Perspective with Curiosity

Next, let's talk about curiosity and openness. Start engaging with people who hold different perspectives, ideas, and backgrounds. Yes, it's way easier to stay in your comfort zone with your like-minded pals but challenge yourself to listen to someone with a different point of view. Instead of rushing to judge or dismiss them, try to understand where they're coming from. Say you find yourself talking with someone who's weirdly obsessed with competitive hot dog eating—something you have no interest in whatsoever (and honestly, kind of makes you gag a little). Rather than writing them off as a walking red flag, get curious. Ask what it is they love about it. You might be surprised to find common ground. Maybe they admire the intense focus and stamina it takes to consume sixty hot dogs in ten minutes (because that's some kind of discipline), kind of like the commitment you bring to your morning yoga practice. Or maybe their unbridled enthusiasm when describing the "dunking technique" reminds you of the way you light up when talking about your favorite books.

But—*and this is important*—this doesn't mean you need to give time or energy to people whose views are dehumanizing or harmful to certain groups of people. You can engage in open-minded conversations without supporting harmful beliefs. When you broaden your understanding of others, you realize that truth is like a patchwork quilt—it's made up of different pieces from different experiences, and you can't see the full picture unless you're open to all the colors. And, no, this doesn't mean you have to agree with everyone all the time. It just means you're expanding your mind and letting life be a little less "us versus them."

And let's not forget about challenging your own assumptions and beliefs. Ask yourself why you believe what you do. Are your beliefs based on solid evidence, or did they come from somewhere like your childhood, a meme you saw on Instagram, or a random conversation with a stranger at a coffee shop? Maybe what fascinates the competitive hot dog eater is the mental strategy behind it—the pacing, the breath control, the way competitors train their bodies to override discomfort. And hey, that kind of mind-body mastery isn't so different from how you prep for a big presentation or regulate your nerves before a tough conversation. Or maybe their eyes light up with the same passion you feel when you talk about your latest creative project.

Be willing to question your assumptions and revise your views in light of new information. Flexibility and adaptability—being open to change—are key when it comes to embracing the gray. Life's not a rulebook. It's a choose-your-own-adventure novel, and the plot twists are way more fun when you're open to them.

Embracing the Present to Find Clarity

Mindfulness is a powerful tool to use to break free from dichotomous habits. When we practice being present in the moment, we stop getting stuck in rigid expectations of how things "should" be or rehashing past mistakes. Mindfulness helps us accept the gray areas of life by teaching us to embrace what is, right here and now. Instead of stressing about the past or future, we cultivate gratitude for the little moments— the sunset, a belly laugh with friends, or that moment of peace when you're alone with your thoughts (and maybe a cup of coffee). Those are the nuances that make life rich and meaningful.

Embracing the gray doesn't mean abandoning your core values or principles. (You're not about to buy a ticket to the next competitive hot dog eating event.) It means acknowledging that life is a lot more complicated and beautiful than we sometimes give it credit for. It's about being humble enough to admit that we don't have all the answers and being open enough to explore and grow from the richness that exists in the gray areas. So, no, it's not about "throwing away" your values—it's about expanding them to include more of what makes life interesting and real.

***

By working on letting go of black-and-white thinking, you're opening up to a world of possibilities. Life becomes less about doing it perfectly and more about living fully—with all the ups, downs, twists, turns, and surprises along the way. When you embrace the messiness of life, you step into your own power and resilience. You'll find that you can hold your truth while also holding space for others to do the same. And that, my friend, is where the magic happens.

11

You Will Be Handed a Shit Sandwich

We've all been there. You pick up a self-help book, attend a workshop, or scroll through Instagram and see motivational quotes and success stories. The message is "If I just do X, Y, and Z, then my life will be easier. I'll be happier, more successful, and finally free from all this chaos." It's a seductive idea, right? The notion that there's a formula out there that, if followed to the letter, will magically turn your life into a smooth, drama-free ride.

But let's be real for a hot minute: Life doesn't work that way. No matter how many morning routines you perfect, how much meditation you practice, or how many vision boards you create, curveballs will inevitably be thrown at you. You will be handed what I like to call "a shit sandwich," and often you won't know what to do with said metaphorical sandwich. It's not a matter of if but when. Life is messy, unpredictable, and often downright unfair. And here's the kicker—we are *not* meant to have an easy life. That's not what we're built for.

You know what we *are* built for? Resilience. Strength. Courage. The ability to get back up when life knocks us down. That's what personal development is really about—not avoiding the shit sandwiches life serves up but learning how to face them head-on with grace, grit, and a little bit of humor. The problem is, sometimes we buy into this idea that if we just follow the right steps, we can sidestep the messiness altogether. We're led to believe that if things aren't going smoothly, we're doing something wrong. And that belief? It's a trap.

When we buy into the illusion of an easy life, we set ourselves up for disappointment. We start to think that we're failing when things get hard, that we're not good enough because we're struggling. Instead of facing the challenges head-on, we start to avoid them. We turn to hyperproductivity, trying to outrun our problems by keeping busy. Or we look to others to take care of us, hoping they can fix things for us. But here's the truth: No one can rescue you from your own life. Only you can do that.

What Happens If You Attempt to Run Away?

Let's talk about the impact of running away as an avoidance strategy. When you're constantly running from your problems—whether by filling your schedule to the brim or expecting others to pick up the pieces—you're doing more than just avoiding discomfort. You're actually depriving yourself of the opportunity to grow, to build the resilience you need to handle life's inevitable challenges.

Hyperproductivity might feel like a solution in the short term. After all, if you're busy, you don't have to think about what's really going on, right? Plus, productivity is noble... it's a valuable thing that never really gets looked at as a "bad" distraction. It's like thinking you're winning at life because you've mastered the art of answering emails while brushing your teeth. But here's the thing: Even if you do answer emails while brushing your teeth, productivity is a numbing mechanism, just like any other. It distracts you from the real issues, but it doesn't solve them. Eventually, that overpacked schedule and to-do list are going to catch up with you. You'll burn out, and when you do, those problems you've been avoiding will still be there, waiting for you.

Looking at another approach, when you rely on others to take care of you when it comes to your problems, you're giving away your power. For example, if you're avoiding a hard conversation and hoping someone else will just take care of it (or that it will magically disappear), you're sending yourself a message that you're not capable of handling your own life, that you need someone else to swoop in to save you. While it's totally okay (and necessary) to lean on others for support, it's not okay to make them responsible for your happiness or your challenges. When you do that, you're not just avoiding the problem—you're avoiding your own strength.

This pattern of avoidance doesn't just keep you stuck—it also erodes your self-confidence. Every time you run from a challenge or look to someone else to fix things, you reinforce the belief that you can't handle it. Over time, that belief starts to seep into every area of your life. You begin to doubt yourself, to second-guess your decisions, to feel like you're constantly on the edge of failure. It's a vicious cycle, and it keeps you small.

But here's the good news: This cycle can be broken. You can stop running. You can face the challenges in your life head-on and come out stronger on the other side. You can access the resilience that's already within you—it's just a matter of learning how to tap into it faster than you panic.

How to Build Tools and Strategies for Better Resilience

So, how do we do it? How do we stop sprinting away from our problems and start facing them with courage and resilience? Let's dive into some tools and strategies that will help you find that strength within yourself.

Practice Realistic Positivity

First up, let's talk about "realistic positivity." Now, I'm all for a positive mindset, but I'm not talking about slapping a smile on your face and pretending everything is sunshine and rainbows when it's not. Realistic positivity is about acknowledging the challenges you're facing while also recognizing your ability to overcome them. It's about saying, "This situation sucks, but I know I can handle it. I've dealt with hard stuff before, and I'll get through this too."

This kind of mindset is powerful because it's rooted in truth. It doesn't deny the reality and discomfort of your situation, but it also doesn't let that reality define you. It's a balanced perspective that allows you to face challenges head-on without falling into the trap of either toxic positivity (ignoring or bypassing the problem) or catastrophic thinking (believing the problem is insurmountable).

To practice realistic positivity, start by naming the challenge you're facing. Say it out loud or write it down. Then remind yourself of a time when you faced a similar challenge and came out on the other side. What did you learn from that experience? How did you grow? Use those memories as proof that you have the resilience to get through whatever you're facing now.

Face It and Own the Outcome

Sometimes when we're handed a shit sandwich and face it, the outcome doesn't go as planned. Using the same example from above, say you've been avoiding that hard conversation, and you decide to call on your courage and do it. But you hesitate, worrying it might go sideways, the other person won't respond in the most mature way, and you'll walk away feeling worse.

The truth is, that might happen.

I can't promise you that things will always work out when you're courageous. Shit sandwiches sometimes bring their friends. But the reality also exists that *you will survive that too*. Yes, it will be uncomfortable. Yes, you won't like it. And yes, you'll learn a lesson from it, *and* the win can be that you went after it instead of ignoring it or having someone do it for you. Setting yourself up for success means that you showed up for your life in this regard, so you can't lose.

Find Your Resilience Role Models

Next, let's talk about role models. I want you to think about the people in your life—or even public figures—who embody resilience. These are the people who have faced significant challenges and come out stronger on the other side. They've been through the fire and have the scars to prove it, but those scars haven't diminished them—they've made them more powerful.

Identify these resilience role models and study their behavior. What qualities do they possess that you admire? How do they handle adversity? What can you learn from their experiences? (If you can't think of anyone, what do you assume are the attributes of a resilience role model?)

Just as importantly, I want you to consider the behaviors you *don't* want to emulate. Maybe you know someone who's gone through a tough time but emerged bitter, angry, or closed off. You know, the type who treats every minor inconvenience like it's a personal attack from the universe—as if the coffee shop running out of oat milk is somehow part of an elaborate cosmic conspiracy against them. Use those examples as a guide for what you want to avoid.

Having resilience role models gives you a blueprint for how to navigate your own challenges. It shows you that it's possible to face difficult situations and not just survive them but thrive because of them. And it reminds you that you're not alone—others have walked this path before you and made it through. You can too.

Embrace Common Humanity by Connecting and Sharing

Another powerful tool for building resilience is embracing the concept of common humanity. When we're going through a tough time, it's easy to feel isolated, like we're the only ones struggling. But the truth is, everyone faces challenges. Everyone goes through periods of pain, loss, and difficulty. It's a universal part of the human experience.

When you embrace this idea of common humanity, you stop seeing your challenges as personal failures and start seeing them as part of what it means to be human. This shift in perspective can be incredibly freeing. It takes the pressure off of you to be perfect, lessens the feelings of loneliness, and allows you to see your struggles as part of the shared journey we're all on.

- **Find your people.** Think of one or two trusted friends, a support group, or even an online community where people have been through similar struggles. If you're not sure where to start, look up forums, local meetups, or even books/podcasts by people who have shared their stories.
- **Take the first step.** Instead of waiting for the "perfect moment," reach out today. Send a text like, "Hey, I've been struggling with [your challenge] and would love to talk. Have you ever been through something similar?" Or if that feels too vulnerable, start by sharing something small and see how they respond.
- **Listen and learn.** When someone opens up to you, resist the urge to compare or "fix" their situation. Just listen. You'll start to see that you're truly not alone—and that connection itself is healing.

There's strength in knowing that you're not alone, that others have been where you are and have found a way through. It's a reminder that you, too, can navigate whatever life throws your way.

Find a Sense of Humor

Finally, let's talk about humor. Yes, humor—even in the face of life's challenges. It might seem counterintuitive, but finding a way to laugh even in the darkest moments is one of the most powerful tools for building resilience. Humor doesn't make the problems go away, but it does change how you relate to them. It lightens the load, if only for a moment, and gives you a fresh perspective.

Think about it: When you're able to find something funny in a tough situation, it shifts your energy. It breaks the cycle of stress and anxiety, even if just for a second. That shift can be enough to give you the strength to keep going. (Ahem, why do you think I'm referring to challenges as "shit sandwiches"?)

So, how do you find humor in difficult times? Start by not taking life too seriously. Allow yourself to see the absurdity in the situation you're struggling in. Maybe it's a string of bad luck that's so ridiculous it's almost comical, or a challenge that's so over-the-top that you can't help but laugh at the sheer craziness of it all. Whatever it is, lean into that humor. Let it be a release valve for the pressure you're feeling.

***

Resilience isn't about never facing challenges. It's about how you respond to them. It's about finding that strength within yourself faster than the panic can set in. The tools I've shared—realistic positivity, resilience role models, common humanity, and humor—are all ways to access that inner strength. They're ways to remind yourself that you're built for this.

12

Believe You Were Meant for and Deserve More

There's a common trope in the land of personal growth that says your beliefs shape your reality; that whatever you believe about things—especially your future and what's possible—will always become your reality. For example, if you believe you're a failure, you will consistently experience defeat.

The truth is, believing you're one thing, such as a failure, does not automatically guarantee that you'll fail. (It does, however, feel like shit.)

Even so, sometimes what we believe about ourselves can dictate how we move through life. And here's the kicker—so many of those beliefs are based on stories we've made up in our heads, stories that aren't necessarily true.

As humans, we're wired to attach meaning to everything. It's part of how we make sense of the world. But sometimes this meaning-making machine goes into overdrive, and we start creating narratives that do more harm than good. You've likely been here before—the stories that start with a simple event, like a coworker giving you a weird look or someone not texting you back right away, and spiral into full-blown catastrophes in your mind.

"He didn't smile at me today or even make eye contact. He must think I'm an idiot."

"She didn't text me back. She must be mad at me."

"I didn't get that promotion. I must be terrible at my job. Maybe I'll get fired soon."

Sound familiar? These stories often come from a place of past experiences and the hurts that came with them. They come from fear and insecurity, and they're fueled by our deep-seated need for validation, approval, and ultimately love. The problem is, when we let these stories run wild and essentially steal the show, we're not just reacting to what's happening in our lives—we're reacting specifically to our fears and insecurities. And that can keep us stuck, spinning in circles, never moving forward.

But here's the truth: Most of these stories aren't true. They're just thoughts—thoughts that have no basis in reality unless we decide to believe them. And that's where things get tricky. If you believe you're bad at your job, or that no one loves you, or that you're not capable of achieving your goals and dreams, then guess what? At best, you're adding a seven-hundred-pound weight on your back as you climb the hill to your goals. At worst, you'll end up exactly as what and where your made-up stories tell you. It's like trying to run a marathon while carrying a grand piano—technically possible but probably not the best strategy unless you're really into extreme musical workouts.

We live in a world that constantly tells us what we should believe—about ourselves, about others, about what's possible. We're bombarded with messages about who we're supposed to be and what our lives should look like. It's easy to get caught up in that, to start believing that we have to fit into a certain mold, that we have to follow a certain path, or that we're not good enough if we don't measure up.

But those beliefs? They're just stories too. And they're stories that can keep us from seeing what's truly possible for our lives.

What Happens If You Believe Your Own Stories?

So, what happens when we believe these stories? When we buy into the idea that we're not good enough, that we'll never get what we want, that our dreams are out of reach? The impact can be profound and far-reaching, touching every aspect of our lives.

First and foremost, these stories limit us. They keep us small, trapped in a box of our own making. When you believe that you're not capable of achieving something, you likely won't even start. And if you do, you'll be regularly scanning for evidence that it won't work. You'll convince yourself that it's not worth the effort, that you're destined to fail, that it's just not in the cards for you. And so you stay stuck, playing it safe, never daring to reach for more because you've already decided it's not possible.

These stories also shape the way we allow others to treat us. If you believe that you're not worthy of love or respect, you'll tolerate behavior that reinforces that belief. You'll stay in toxic relationships, put up with mistreatment, and settle for less than you deserve because you don't believe you deserve any better. Many times, it's not a case of consciously thinking to yourself, *I'm not worthy of anything better, so I'll settle for this crappy relationship.* No, it's typically an unconscious belief that's sneaky. Over time, these beliefs—conscious or unconscious—erode your sense of self-worth even further, creating a vicious cycle of negative self-belief and negative experiences.

And let's not forget how these stories impact our decision-making. When you're operating from a place of fear and limitation, every choice you make is influenced by those beliefs. You'll shy away from opportunities, avoid taking risks, and prioritize safety over growth. You'll say no to things that could expand your horizons simply because you can't see beyond the limited stories you've told yourself about what's possible.

Perhaps the most insidious impact of these stories is the way they keep us disconnected from our true potential. When you believe you're not capable, not enough, you lose touch with that inner fire, that sense of possibility that drives you to pursue your dreams. You stop dreaming altogether because you've convinced yourself that it's pointless. And that, my friend, is the biggest tragedy of all.

How to Start Believing in Possibility

Alright, enough with the doom and gloom. It's time to flip the script and start believing in and rooting for what's possible. Because here's the truth: You are capable, you are plenty enough, and your dreams are absolutely within reach. But to make them a reality, you first have to believe they're even remotely achievable. So, let's dive into some tools and strategies to help you cut through the bullshit stories and start seeing what's truly possible for your life.

Identify the Stories You're Telling Yourself

The first step in changing your beliefs is to become aware of the stories you're telling yourself. This requires self-reflection and honesty because some of these stories might be so ingrained that you don't even realize they're there.

Start by paying attention to your thoughts, especially when you're faced with a challenge or a setback. What's the first thing that comes to mind? Do you immediately jump to conclusions about your abilities or the outcome? Do you start spinning a narrative about how you're doomed to fail or how things never work out for you?

When you catch yourself in these thought patterns, take a step back and ask yourself, *Is this really true? Or is this just a story I'm telling myself?*

At first this can be hard to remember in the moment—especially if you're used to getting swept up in these thoughts without even realizing it. To help train yourself, try setting a reminder on your phone a few times a day to pause and check in. When the alert goes off, take a deep breath and reflect on how your thoughts have been going so far. Have you been telling yourself a story that may not be entirely true?

Another way to build this habit is to tie it to something you already do daily—like brushing your teeth, making coffee, or getting in your car. Use that moment as a cue to ask yourself, *What story am I telling myself right now? And is it really the truth?* The more you practice, the more automatic it becomes.

Once you've built this awareness, challenge the validity of these thoughts. *Where did they come from? Are they based on facts, or are they fueled by fear and insecurity?* At this point in the process, you're not trying to change the story or your inner dialogue—you're simply getting *curious*. By questioning these stories, you start to loosen their grip on you, creating space for new, more empowering beliefs to take root.

Get Some Big Prize Energy

When I decided to leave my marriage early in 2023, I walked away feeling sad and defeated. This was my second marriage, and I spent some time in the depths of despair deciding that I was a failure at marriage, relationships in general, and thus at life.

However, I didn't spend much time there.

I quickly saw that those beliefs would not serve me. Yes, I needed to go through the grief of my marriage ending, but as that subsided (and if you've ever ended a marriage or long relationship, you know that the grief can happen long before you actually split up), I decided to try on another perspective. I decided I needed to change the story about who I was. So, I decided that I was the prize. I called it "Big Prize Energy."

I made a playlist of songs that represented this energy, but more importantly, I made a list of behaviors that represented Big Prize Energy. I asked myself, *What would someone who truly leaned into knowing they were THE Prize do, have, and feel? What would she believe is possible for her life? What stories about herself would she believe, and which ones would she reject?*

So, what are yours? If you were to wake up one morning and all of the other disempowering stories you've made up about yourself were gone and replaced with stories and beliefs that you are THE Prize, how would your life change?

Spend some time reflecting and journaling on your own Big Prize Energy. If you're inspired by what you find there, commit to action steps!

Defining Your Own "More"

Now that you've started clearing away the limiting beliefs and external expectations, it's time to get crystal clear on what "more" means for you. Because here's the truth: What's possible for you is as unique as you are, and it's up to you to define what that looks like.

"More" could mean a lot of different things. It could mean more joy, more success, more love, more freedom. It could mean pursuing a passion project, taking a leap of faith in your career, or simply allowing yourself to dream bigger than you ever have before. Whatever it is, it has to come from *you*. It has to be aligned with your values, desires, and vision for your life.

Take some time to really explore what "more" means for you. What would make you feel fulfilled? What would make your heart sing? What would make you excited to jump out of bed in the morning? Write it down, visualize it, feel it in your bones. If you're unsure, think about what you want *less* of in your life, and that may help point you to what you want more of. The clearer you are on what you want, the easier it will be to believe that it's possible.

Set Boundaries Around How Others Treat You

Let's talk about boundaries. Because a big part of believing in what's possible for your life is about how you allow others to treat you. If you're constantly letting people walk all over you, if you're tolerating behavior that undermines your self-worth, it's going to be a hell of a lot harder to believe in your own potential.

Setting boundaries isn't about being harsh or unkind—it's about respecting yourself enough to say, "This is what I will accept, and this is what I won't. Period." It's like having a bouncer for your life, except instead of checking IDs, they're checking if people's behavior passes the "not testing my patience" test. It's about surrounding yourself with people who lift you up, who support your dreams, and who believe in your potential as much as you do. And it's about cutting ties (with kindness) with those who don't, because you don't have the time or energy to spend on relationships that keep you small.

Step 1: Get clear on your nonnegotiables. What are the behaviors or attitudes you will not tolerate in your life? What are the standards you want to uphold for how you're treated? Get honest with yourself and write these down so you have a clear reference point.

Step 2: Communicate your boundaries clearly. Once you know what your boundaries are, speak them out loud. Communicate them clearly and confidently—whether it's with a partner, friend, colleague, or family member.

Step 3: Reinforce your boundaries when they're tested. Setting boundaries is an ongoing process—it's something you will need to revisit and reinforce as you grow and evolve. People might test your boundaries, intentionally or unintentionally, and that's your opportunity to reaffirm them. Setting boundaries isn't a one-and-done deal—it's a practice. They're about showing up for yourself consistently and reminding the world (and yourself) that you were meant for and deserve more.

Every time you set and enforce a boundary, you're sending yourself a powerful message. You're saying, *I deserve to be treated with respect, and I'm committed to standing up for what I need.* That's how you start believing in what's possible for your life—by creating an environment where your worth is honored, your values are supported, and your energy is protected.

Setting boundaries isn't just an act of self-respect; it's an act of self-love. It creates space for you to grow, to dream, and to step into the version of yourself that you've always been capable of becoming. And that, my friend, is the kind of environment where anything becomes possible.

The stories we tell ourselves can either propel us forward or keep us stuck in a cycle of fear and limitation. By recognizing the untrue narratives that we've been living by, we can rewrite them and make space for more empowered beliefs. When you start to believe that your dreams are within reach—that you're worthy of love, success, and happiness—you'll begin to show up in a way that reflects that. When you do this, you're living like you give a damn about your own potential. Your story isn't set in stone—it's yours to reshape. So stand up, shake off those doubts, and start believing in something bigger than the limitations you've accepted. Time to write your own damn story and make it count.

13

Rush the Net

As a child, I spent a lot of time on the tennis court. My dad was an avid player, and much of his social circle was involved with tennis. I started playing when I was about four years old, and for many years, my dad was my tennis coach.

"Whenever you can, even if you're afraid, rush the net. When you see an opportunity, don't hesitate—charge forward," he'd tell me. He taught me the advantages of this strategy. I remember him telling me that when you use this game plan, especially in the beginning, your opponent knows you're not afraid of "aggressive" strategies. At the time, I thought it was just about tennis, but as I've gotten older, I've realized those lessons were about much more than winning or even sports.

This lesson boils down to this core idea: Show up to life with confidence and the willingness to take risks, even when it's scary. Rushing the net says, *I'm going after what I want, no matter how it turns out.* And *If you're going to play with me, be prepared for me to take this game into my own hands, because I know what I'm doing.* Confidence isn't about guaranteeing success but rather having the courage to show up fully and take the shot.

Taking the time to intentionally build courage and confidence is one of the keys to living like you give a damn.

Whether you're walking into a boardroom, stepping into a tough conversation, or chasing a dream, confidence is the thing that allows you to go for it—even when you don't feel ready. It's not magic or luck; it's a skill you can build. Just like rushing the net, it starts with making bold moves, no matter how small.

So, let's dive into what's holding you back, what's at stake if you don't take action, and how to build the kind of confidence that will make you want to charge forward in every area of your life.

What Happens If Fear Holds the Racket?

Confidence can feel elusive, right? Like some people were just born with it, while others, well, weren't. But the truth is, confidence isn't a personality trait—it's a skill. Yet so many of us hold ourselves back, believing we need to feel confident *before* we take action.

Here's the real problem: We're taught to avoid failure at all costs. Society, our families, and even our own brains condition us to play it safe, avoid mistakes, and stick to what we know. As a result, we stop taking risks. We let fear of failure—or even fear of success—hold us back. This mindset is a confidence killer because confidence grows through action and experience. Without action, our confidence can't thrive.

You might recognize this in your own life. Maybe you hesitate to speak up in meetings, fearing your ideas aren't good enough. Maybe you've dreamed of starting a business, traveling the world, or making a big life change, but the voice in your head says, *What if I fail?* You don't even let yourself try. Instead, you settle for safe, familiar patterns.

Imagine standing on the baseline in a tennis match. (Or pickleball, because who doesn't want a sport that's basically Ping-Pong on steroids?) You see your opponent do the exact things you've been taught to look for when you'll have a perfect opportunity to rush the net and score the point.

But instead of charging forward, you hesitate. You stay back, telling yourself it's safer to wait. The play continues, and the opportunity is gone. You've lost the point.

That's what life looks like when you don't build confidence or take risks. You play small. You stay in your comfort zone. And over time, this hesitation costs you.

What Playing Small Looks Like in Real Life

We don't always realize when we're playing small. It's sneaky, often disguised as practicality, overpreparing, or waiting for the "right time." But if you're constantly holding yourself back out of fear—fear of failure, rejection, or simply being *too much*—then you're keeping yourself stuck.

So, what does playing small actually look like in real life?

- **In your career:** You stay in a job that is a soul-sucker because you're afraid you won't succeed in something new. You don't ask for the raise or promotion because you worry you'll be seen as "too much" or you don't meet every single qualification.
- **In relationships:** You settle for what feels safe rather than what sets your heart on fire. You hold back from being vulnerable because it feels risky to show your whole self.
- **In your dreams:** You stay stuck in the research and planning phase, endlessly preparing but never taking the leap.

What's the cost? Missed opportunities. Unlived dreams. A life that feels smaller than it could be. Confidence doesn't just show up one day like an unexpected package on your doorstep. It's built through the very risks you're avoiding.

But what if you *have* taken the leap before and it didn't go as planned? Maybe you put yourself out there, made the big move, started the thing—and it didn't work out the way you hoped. That experience might have left you hesitant, questioning if it's even worth trying again. Here's the truth: Setbacks don't mean you weren't capable. They don't mean you're doomed to fail again. Every risk—even the ones that don't pan out—holds valuable information about what worked, what didn't, and what you might do differently next time. The real danger isn't in failing; it's in letting one disappointment become the reason you never try again.

Taking another leap doesn't mean ignoring what happened before but rather using it as fuel to move forward *smarter, stronger, and braver than before.*

How to "Rush the Net" and Build Confidence

Here's the good news: Confidence is a skill you can learn. And even better, science shows us exactly how to build it. Dr. Ian Robertson, a neuroscientist and clinical psychologist, has researched confidence extensively. He describes it as a "circuit" in your brain—a process you can strengthen with practice.

The Five Principles of Building Confidence

Let's break down Dr. Robertson's research into five actionable principles you can use right now to start building your confidence.[1]

1. **Action creates confidence.** Confidence doesn't come first; action does. When you take action—no matter how small—you show your brain that you're capable, and your brain rewards you with a dopamine boost. This positive feedback loop builds momentum.
   Action step: Choose one small, scary action you've been avoiding. Maybe it's speaking up in a meeting, starting a conversation with someone new, or finally hitting "publish" on that social

media post. Take the step and notice how it shifts your energy. Journal on it, and tell someone about it who you know will celebrate with you.

2. **Celebrate your wins.** Your brain is wired to focus on failure more than success—it's a survival mechanism. But you can counteract this by consciously celebrating your wins, no matter how small.

   Action step: At the end of each day, write down *one thing* you did well. Over time, this trains your brain to notice your strengths instead of fixating on your flaws.

3. **Visualize success.** Athletes have used visualization for decades to prepare for success. Studies show that mentally rehearsing a positive outcome primes your brain to take action. *(It's science!)*

   Action step: Spend five minutes visualizing yourself succeeding in a situation that scares you or that you think isn't possible. Picture the details—what you're wearing, how you're feeling, and how others respond. Let your brain experience the win before it happens.

4. **Surround yourself with confidence builders.** Confidence is contagious. The people you spend time with have a profound impact on how you see yourself.

   Action step: Identify one person who inspires you with their confidence and reach out to them. Whether it's asking for advice, spending time together, or even just observing how they carry themselves, their energy will rub off on you.

5. **Reframe nervousness as excitement.** When you're nervous, your body's physical response—racing heart, sweaty palms, shallow breath—is almost identical to excitement.

By reframing the feeling, you can turn fear into a confidence boost.

Action step: The next time you feel nervous, tell yourself, *I'm excited to do this*. Notice how it shifts your mindset. You don't have to convince yourself you're not nervous. Both things can (and will) exist together, but focus on the excitement more.

Powerful Questions to Uncover Your Self-Doubt

Confidence starts with awareness. You can't address or be what you don't see, so let's get clear on what's holding you back. Take a moment to reflect on the following questions. Get out your favorite journal or note-taking app and ask yourself:

- *What's one area of my life where I'm holding back because of fear or self-doubt?*
- *What would it look like to take bold action in that area?*
- *What's the worst that could happen if I fail? And if I did, how would I bounce back?*
- *What's the best that could happen if I succeed?*
- *When was a time that I felt truly confident? What was I doing? What did that feel like?*
- *Who benefits when I stay small? Who suffers?*

These questions aren't about blaming yourself for playing small. They're about shining a light on the areas where you're ready to grow. Clarity is power, and the answers to these questions can help you take your first bold step.

Why Risk-Taking Is the Key to Confidence

Rushing the net doesn't guarantee a win. Sometimes you'll miss the shot and even lose the game. (Like that time I tried to impress someone with a tennis serve and hit myself in the face—not exactly a confidence-building moment, but hey, at least I learned how *not* to serve.) But every time you charge forward, you're proving to yourself that you're capable of taking the risk. Every time you charge forward, you're telling the people who are watching that you know it's possible and that you're willing to go for it. Every time you charge forward, you are betting on yourself. Confidence isn't about always succeeding—it's about knowing you have what it takes to try.

Just as important, risk-taking builds resilience. It trains your brain to see failure as a stepping stone, not an endpoint. The more risks you take, the more evidence you gather that you can handle whatever comes your way.

***

Confidence isn't about never being afraid. It's about showing up anyway, with your shaky hands and racing heart, and taking action. It's about rushing the net—not because you know you'll win or you're fearless against any "opponent" but because the game is worth playing.

So, here's your challenge: Take one small, bold action today. Answer the questions in the chapter. Take the risk. Because confidence isn't something you wait for—it's something you create. The life you're dreaming of is waiting for you to show up and claim it.

14

People Who Hurt You Can Be Your Greatest Teachers

Let me take you back to my early thirties when I was deep in the aftermath of two back-to-back relationships that nearly broke me. You know how it feels when you think you've finally found "the one," only to have it blow up in your face? Not once, but twice? Yeah, that was me. I was devastated, crushed by betrayal and disappointment. I felt like I'd given everything—my love, my time, my effort—only to be left in pieces.

Looking back now, I realize that those relationships were some of my greatest teachers. The pain I went through became the very thing that lit a fire under me to rebuild myself, not just for someone else but for *me*. And that's what I want to talk about: how to take situations where you've been hurt, betrayed, or abandoned, and spin that pain into your biggest source of motivation.

Holding on to hurt, bitterness, and resentment is like carrying a heavy weight and expecting someone else to feel the burden. It doesn't work. All that pain you carry? It weighs you down, keeps you stuck, and blinds you to the lessons that are right there in front of you. You get caught in the cycle of *Why did this happen to me?* instead of asking, *What is this here to teach me?* And that shift in perspective can change everything.

But I get it. When you're in the thick of it, when you've been hurt by someone you trusted, it's so much easier to hang on to the anger, the sadness, the frustration. It feels safer than admitting that maybe you ignored the red flags, that you compromised too much, or that you walked away from your own needs just to stay in the relationship. But if we're going to grow from our pain, we have to be willing to face those hard truths.

What Happens If Bitterness and Self-Abandonment Are Impacting You?

Let's talk about what happens when you hold on to that hurt. When you carry that bitterness with you like armor, thinking it's protecting you from getting hurt again, it's actually doing the opposite. It's keeping you from fully living, from fully loving, and from fully trusting yourself. Worst of all, it keeps you stuck in the past, replaying the same hurt over and over again instead of moving forward.

When we don't process our pain, it shows up in other areas of our lives. Maybe you've become cynical about love, convinced that every relationship is doomed to fail. Or maybe you still want a relationship but you've stopped putting yourself out there because the fear of being hurt again is just too much to bear. Or maybe you're stuck in a current relationship that doesn't feel good but you can't seem to leave because deep down, you believe this is the best you're going to get.

Sound familiar? When we don't address the hurt, when we don't turn inward to ask ourselves what we *really* need, we end up essentially walking away from ourselves over and over again. We stay in jobs we hate, friendships that drain us, and relationships that don't serve us—even our relationship with our own self-worth—because we've convinced ourselves that this is as good as it gets.

The problem with bitterness is that it makes you feel like you're taking control, like holding on to the pain is somehow protecting you from future harm. But in reality it's just keeping you tethered to the very thing that hurt you in the first place. You're allowing that pain to take up space in your life when what you really need is to make space for healing, growth, and the lessons that come from it.

Here's the tough-love part: Every time you stay in that hurt, every time you let bitterness run the show, you're turning your back on yourself. You're saying to yourself, *My pain is more important than my peace. My resentment is more important than my future happiness.* And let's be real—bitterness is like that one houseguest who swore they were just staying for the weekend but is somehow still on your couch three months later, eating your snacks and complaining about the Wi-Fi. Time to hand them a suitcase and show them the door.

How to Turn Your Hurt into Motivation

Okay, enough with the heavy stuff. It's time to talk about how to turn things around to live like you give a damn. Because while the hurt you've experienced is real, so is your power to use it for something greater. Pain can be your greatest source of wisdom if you let it, and the key to doing that is learning how to take those experiences and turn them into your teachers. Here's how.

Facing the Truth About What You Ignored, Dismissed, or Compromised

The first step to turning your hurt into motivation is to get really honest with yourself. This is where some tough questions come in, and I'm going to ask you to sit with these, journal on them, and dig deep. So, get out a piece of paper or your favorite note-taking app, and let's get to work.

- *What did I ignore or dismiss in that relationship?* Were there red flags you waved away because you wanted the relationship to work so badly? Did you stay silent when you should've spoken up? Did you compromise on something important to you because you were afraid of losing the other person?
- *Where did I abandon myself to stay in the relationship?* Did you give up parts of yourself—your dreams, your voice, your values—just to keep the peace? Did you prioritize their happiness over your own, hoping that if you made them happy enough, they wouldn't leave?
- *What was I trying to prove, and to whom?* Were you trying to prove you were lovable, worthy, or good enough? Were you trying to show other people (or maybe yourself) that you could make this relationship work, no matter what it cost you?

These questions may be hard. They force you to look at the ways you may have turned your back on yourself. But here's the thing: Acknowledging this isn't about blaming yourself for what happened. It's about empowering yourself to take responsibility for your healing and growth. Once you see where you may have compromised yourself, you can make damn sure you never do it again.

Learning the Lessons—Reframing the Pain

Now that you've identified what went wrong and where you may have walked away from yourself, it's time to reframe the pain. Every difficult relationship, every heartbreak, has the opportunity to hold a mirror up to you—if you're willing to look closely and learn from it.

Ask yourself:

- *What did this experience teach me about myself?*
- *What did it reveal about what I need in a relationship or in life?*
- *How can I use this pain as a reminder of what I deserve and what I will no longer tolerate?*

When you start to see your pain as a teacher instead of something to avoid or bury, you begin to reclaim your power. When you're ready, you can shift from feeling like a victim of your circumstances to being the hero of your own story. You realize that every single hurt has given you the gift of clarity—clarity about who you are, what you want, and what you're willing to fight for in your life.

Finding Motivation in the Pain—Fueling Your Future

Now that you've reframed the pain, it's time to use it as fuel. The hurt you've been through doesn't have to hold you back—it can be the very thing that pushes you forward. Think about it: All that energy you've spent holding on to bitterness? Imagine what could happen if you redirected that energy toward your own growth and healing.

Here's what's possible: Take everything you've learned from the hurt, everything that relationship showed you about what you deserve, and use it as motivation. Use it as the reason you're going to bet on yourself from now on. (Remember chapter 8?) This pain? It's not your enemy. It's your rocket fuel. Use it as the fire that fuels you to never walk away from yourself again.

So, if you're wondering how to turn all that hurt into motivation—look no further than your own story. Remember those two back-to-back relationships I mentioned from my early thirties, the ones that nearly broke me in the moment? All these years later, they've turned out to be my greatest teachers. The pain I experienced wasn't just something to be endured; it was something to be learned from. It showed me the parts of myself I needed to reclaim and the boundaries I needed to strengthen. It gave me clarity about who I want to be and what I'll no longer tolerate. And now, as I stand here wiser and infinitely stronger, I can tell you without a doubt that the hurt you've gone through has the potential to shape you into the most resilient, authentic version of yourself—if you let it.

Remembering Your Worth

I want to leave you with one final reminder, and it's the most important one: You have always been loved. Even in your darkest moments, when it felt like no one cared, when you were drowning in the aftermath of heartbreak, you were loved—divinely, through other people, and most importantly by yourself.

Maybe you forgot that for a while. Maybe you've been so focused on the pain that you've lost sight of the love that's always been there, waiting for you to come back to it. But it's never too late. You've always been worthy of love simply because you exist. And the love you've been looking for? It's been within you all along.

***

So go out there and live your life knowing that you are loved, you are worthy, and you are so much stronger than you think. The hurt may have shaped you, but it doesn't define you. You get to decide what happens next, and I know, without a doubt, that what comes next is going to be amazing.

15

Treat Your Trauma with Respect

Let's get real right off the bat. I know you didn't pick up this book to get hit with a chapter on trauma. You're here for some inspiration, maybe a bit of ass-kicking motivation. But trauma? That's heavy stuff, right? Trust me, I get it. We don't exactly sit around at brunch with our friends and say, "You know what? I think I'm ready to dive headfirst into my deepest, darkest pain today." No, we avoid it like the plague because it's messy and uncomfortable. And frankly, it hurts.

But here's the kicker: Avoiding trauma doesn't make it disappear. It's not like that awkward text you didn't respond to that will just go away if you ignore it long enough. It's like that bad haircut you got in seventh grade—you can try to hide it with hats and creative styling, but those tragic school photos are eternal proof that, yes, you really did think a mullet-mohawk combo was a good idea.

Trauma has a way of showing up in all the corners of your life, even if you've shoved it into the farthest back drawer of your mind. Trauma impacts the nervous system like a piano that's been dropped. Some keys are stuck, others are too sensitive, and the harmony is way off or gone. With time and care, the piano can be tuned and restored, but it requires patience to bring the music back.

Trauma follows you into your relationships, your job, your parenting. Most importantly, it seeps into how you see yourself and the world around you.

And what does that look like? Maybe you're in a relationship and find yourself getting irrationally angry or defensive about something small. Maybe you have trust issues, or you struggle with vulnerability because being hurt before taught you that walls are safer than openness. Or perhaps you've got a constant underlying feeling of anxiety or fear that you can't quite pin down. That could be trauma. That's the stuff we think we've buried deep, showing up again and again until we finally face it.

We run from it because we've been taught that pain is bad, and our instinct is to avoid things that make us feel bad. It's totally human. But what if I told you that running from your trauma is exactly what's keeping you stuck? What if I told you that moving toward it—yes, actually facing it—is the ticket to your freedom? Sounds scary, I know, but facing your trauma isn't just about healing your past; it's about unlocking your future.

What Happens If Trauma Isn't Just in the Past?

The sneaky thing about trauma is that it doesn't stay neatly in the past where we think it belongs. It doesn't just hang out deep in the memories of what happened years ago, being still and staying quiet. No, trauma has a way of weaving itself into the fabric of your everyday life even when you don't realize it. If you're sitting here thinking, *But my trauma isn't that big*, or *I've moved past that*, let's chat.

Trauma is not just about the big, obvious things—abuse, loss, or major life-altering events. It can be the smaller, cumulative things too: being regularly criticized as a child, feeling neglected emotionally in a relationship, or experiencing a loss of identity after a job or life transition. These experiences can impact how we move through the world, even if we don't think they're "big deals" on the surface. If it hurt you, if it left a mark, it matters.

So how does this show up in your life today? Maybe you're stuck in a cycle of overworking because you're afraid of being seen as not enough. Maybe you can't let yourself relax because, deep down, you believe your worth is wrapped up in your productivity. Maybe you shy away from intimacy because vulnerability feels too risky. Maybe you self-sabotage when things start going well because success feels unfamiliar and uncomfortable.

Here's the thing: Trauma has a way of creating patterns in our lives that can keep us stuck if we're not aware of them. These patterns might look like people-pleasing, perfectionism, avoiding hard conversations or conflict, or even procrastination. Trauma doesn't just live in the past—it shapes your present and can block your future if you don't deal with it.

And here's where it gets tricky: These patterns? They become part of your identity. You start to think, *This is just who I am*, when really it's just how you've learned to cope. But it's not who you are. It's who you've had to be to survive. And that's the good news—because if it's something you learned, it's something you can unlearn.

How to Start Facing Your Trauma and Unlocking Your Future

Let's talk about how to actually move forward. While trauma is heavy and complex, it's also something you can work through. The possibilities on the other side of it? Freedom, growth, and opportunities that you can't even imagine right now.

One of the most exciting concepts in psychology and science is something called post-traumatic growth. Sounds pretty badass, right? Well, it is. Coined by psychologists Richard Tedeschi and Lawrence Calhoun, post-traumatic growth (PTG) is the idea that after experiencing trauma, many people don't just bounce back to where they were—they grow beyond it. They develop a deeper appreciation for life, stronger relationships, and a belief in new possibilities. It's not about being "happy" that the trauma happened but acknowledging that the trauma helped you grow into a version of yourself that is wiser, stronger, and more resilient.

So how do you get there? How do you stop running from your trauma and start using it to fuel your growth? We'll look at six ways to do this, as well as questions to journal and reflect on in order to guide you to new perspectives. So, get out a piece of paper or your favorite note-taking app and let's begin.

Acknowledge Your Trauma

The first step is simple but not easy: You have to acknowledge your trauma. I'm not saying you need to relive it or go through every painful detail, but you have to stop pretending it didn't have the impact it did. Avoiding it only gives it more power. When you acknowledge your trauma and its impact, you take the first step toward taking your power back. This might look like unpacking it with a therapist, looking at old journals, or just taking time to reflect. Ask yourself:

- *What, if anything, am I running from?*
- *How has this trauma shaped the way I see myself or the world?*
- *What patterns, behaviors, or beliefs have I developed because of this experience? In other words, how has it held me back?*

This isn't about blaming anyone or anything—it's about understanding where you are so you can move forward. Be as honest as possible with yourself. These answers are just about collecting information so that you can see where you can grow.

Shift Your Perspective—the Possibility of Growth

Once you've acknowledged the impact of your trauma, it's time to work on shifting your perspective. Instead of seeing your trauma as something that limits you, start to see it as something that can fuel your growth. This is where the concept of post-traumatic growth comes in. Ask yourself:

- *What has this experience taught me about myself?*
- *How has it made me stronger, wiser, or more resilient?*
- *What possibilities does this experience open up for me moving forward?*

You don't have to have all the answers right now, but starting to ask these questions will help you shift from a place of possible stuckness to a place of empowerment.

Embrace Common Humanity

One of the hardest parts of trauma is feeling isolated, like you're the only one going through it. But here's the truth: You're not alone. Everyone—yes, *everyone*—has experienced some form of trauma in their life. It might look different from yours, but pain is universal. When you can embrace this common humanity, it helps take away the shame and isolation that trauma can create.

Find people who have been through similar experiences, whether through support groups, friends, or even reading about others' journeys. Social media can be a great place for this. Knowing that you're not alone is a crucial step in healing. Ask yourself:

- *Is there anything that is holding me back from sharing my story with others?*
- *Who in my life can I share my story with to feel less alone?*
- *What can I learn from hearing about others' experiences with trauma?*

Cultivate Realistic Positivity

I'm all about optimism, but when it comes to trauma, it's important to acknowledge that this might not be the time for going straight to positivity. This isn't about slapping on a smile and pretending everything is fine. It's about acknowledging the pain *and* believing that there's light on the other side of it. Realistic positivity means accepting that healing is hard work, but it's worth it. It means believing in the possibility of growth even when you can't see the full picture yet. Ask yourself:

- *What small signs of progress have I noticed in my healing journey?*
- *How can I balance hope and honesty as I work through this?*
- *What reminders or other support systems can I use to stay motivated on difficult days?*

Keep a Sense of Humor

This might sound a little unexpected but hear me out— keeping a sense of humor can be a surprisingly powerful tool for healing. Trauma is heavy, but finding moments of lightness can help ease the burden. It doesn't mean you're not taking your pain seriously or that you're laughing at yourself—it means you're giving yourself permission to reclaim some joy and perspective. You're simply adding levity to a heavy situation. Humor can help you feel more in control and less overwhelmed, even during the darkest times. Ask yourself:

- *What lighthearted or funny moments can I reflect on that brought me some relief during challenging times?*
- *How can I invite more humor into my life, even during tough times?*
- *What's one absurd or funny aspect of my healing journey that I can laugh about?*

Celebrate Your Progress

Lastly, don't forget to celebrate the small victories along the way. Healing from trauma isn't a straight line—it's a journey, and it takes time. But every step you take toward facing your pain is a step toward your freedom. So celebrate the hell out of that. Give yourself credit for the work you're doing, for the courage it takes to face your trauma head-on, and for the growth that's happening, even if it's slow. Ask yourself:

- *What progress have I made that I'm proud of, no matter how small?*
- *How can I reward myself for the work I'm doing to heal?*
- *Who in my life can I share my victories with to help me celebrate?*

Facing your trauma is no small feat, but it's the key to unlocking your future. By acknowledging your pain, shifting your perspective, and embracing the possibility of growth, you open yourself up to a life of limitless possibilities. The trauma you've experienced doesn't define you. It's simply a part of your story. And you, my friend, are the author of that story. You get to decide how it unfolds.

16

People Will Judge You, and Sometimes They're Just Not That Into You

Judgment and *rejection*—even just those words can make you squirm, right? If so, you're not alone. Science tells us that the same areas of the brain are stimulated when we experience rejection as when we experience physical pain.[1] That's why when you get dumped, ghosted, or left off the group chat for brunch plans, it makes perfect sense to say, "It feels like a punch in the gut." Studies also show that feeling judged and then rejected for it makes us relive and reexperience social pain more vividly than we do physical pain.[2] If you've ever nursed a breakup or not been picked for a team (sports or trivia—no judgment here), you know exactly what I'm talking about. Emotional ouch. When we get judged and rejected, our need to belong is destabilized, and the resulting disconnection adds a cherry on top of our emotional sundae of pain. Fun, right?

Here's the kicker: We live in a world where people are judging all the time. If you've ever been told, "Stop judging others!" let me break it to you: not happening. Ever. Judging is what our brains are wired to do. It's one of the ways we navigate the world—sorting people, things, and experiences into little mental boxes to help us make decisions and stay alive. Back in the day, this kind of judgment kept our ancestors from inviting lions into the cave for dinner. But now? It means we're deciding within seconds if someone is trustworthy, attractive, or just plain annoying.

But let's talk about what happens when this gets tangled up with our self-worth. We've all been there, obsessing over someone else's opinion of us. Maybe it's a coworker who didn't laugh at your joke in the meeting or the mom at school drop-off who gave you a weird look. When we let every raised eyebrow or unreturned text mean something about us, we hand over the keys to our happiness. The real issue is this: We're too busy chasing approval from people who don't matter and not focused enough on the people who do.

Also, let's just rip off this Band-Aid now: Not everyone is going to like you. You already know this, right? Some people won't be into you no matter how many amazing qualities you have. You could be chocolate—a literal gift from the heavens—and someone out there still prefers vanilla. Or worse, no dessert at all. The audacity.

What Happens If You Try to Get Everyone to Like You?

If you don't get a handle on this judgment-and-approval spiral, you'll stay stuck on the world's most exhausting hamster wheel. You'll bend yourself into a pretzel trying to win people over, sacrificing your authenticity and your joy along the way. Not-so-shocking news: It never works. No matter how much you try, you can't please everyone. Someone will always find something about you to criticize, whether it's your haircut, your career choices, or how you pronounce *pecan*. (Seriously, people get *very* opinionated about that one.)

What happens when you live like this? You start to lose yourself. You silence your voice, water yourself down, and make decisions based on what other people think instead of what feels right for you. The worst part? Even when you try to be everything to everyone, rejection still stings. Why? Because you've tied your self-worth to external approval, and now every critical comment or side-eye feels like a direct hit to your soul.

Living for others' opinions also keeps you from going after the things you really want. Worried about what people will think? You might not apply for that dream job, start that side hustle, or wear that bold lipstick shade that makes you feel unstoppable. When fear of judgment holds you back, you end up living a smaller, less exciting life—and let's be real, you deserve *the best*.

How to Let Go of Everyone Liking You

Okay, now that we've ripped apart the problem, let's stitch it back together with solutions that actually work. Here's how you can stop letting judgment and rejection run the show:

Accept That Judging Is Inevitable—Including Your Own

In case you're wondering: Everyone judges. Even you. You might think, *But I'm a nice person! I don't judge people!* Yes, you do. We all do. And that's okay! The goal isn't to stop judging—it's to notice when you're doing it and catch yourself before you spiral. For example, when you see someone wearing something that makes you think, *What are they thinking?* pause and ask yourself, *Why do I care? I'm not wearing it; they are.* That simple question and reframe can snap you out of judgment mode and back into your own lane.

The same goes for worrying about other people judging you. Assume they're doing it (because they are!) and let them. People's opinions are a reflection of their own values and experiences—not your worth. Let them judge. It's not your problem.

Get Clear on Whose Opinions Actually Matter

Not all opinions are created equal. There's a big difference between constructive feedback from someone you trust and a random snarky comment from a stranger on the internet. So, here's your homework: Make a list of the people whose opinions actually matter to you. These should be people who truly care about your well-being and want to see you thrive. Cheat code: This list should be *short*. Like fewer-than-your-fingers short. If someone isn't on that list, it's not that you don't care about them but rather that their judgment doesn't need to take up space in your head.

Embrace That Not Everyone Will Like You—and That's Okay

This one's tough, I know. But it's also liberating. When you accept that some people just won't vibe with you, it frees you to stop trying so hard to win them over. Think of yourself as a unique flavor: Not everyone likes mint chocolate chip, but the people who do, *love it*. You're mint chocolate chip. Or rocky road. Or strawberry swirl. Whatever your flavor, own it. The right people will appreciate you for who you are, quirks and all.

If someone doesn't like you, try not to take it personally. It's not a reflection of your value—it's just a mismatch. Like I said earlier, some people don't even like chocolate. That's not chocolate's fault.

But let's go a little deeper—like *energy deep*. Think of people as vibrating on different frequencies, like radio stations. You've got your own energetic wavelength, and the people who "get" you are those tuned in to a similar frequency. These are your people. They vibe with you because their energy resonates with yours. When you meet someone whose "station" is way off from yours, it's not a sign that you're flawed or that they're a jerk—it just means you're on different wavelengths. It's not good or bad; it's just different.

When you start to see relationships this way, it's easier to let go of the need to force connections. Think about it: You wouldn't try to listen to pop hits on a jazz station, right? You'd just tune to a different station that plays the music you love. People are the same. Stop trying to get AM stations to play your FM jam, and let them do their thing while you do yours.

Here's the magic part: When you lean into your own authentic energy, the people who resonate with it will naturally gravitate toward you. You don't have to chase them, convince them, or prove your worth. They'll just *get* you, and that's the best kind of connection. So, if someone doesn't click with you? Bless and release, my friend. Wish them well on their journey and trust that your path is leading you to your own energetic soul circle.

Build Your Rejection Resilience

Rejection hurts, no doubt about it. But you can learn to bounce back faster. Start by reframing rejection as a redirection. Instead of thinking, *They don't like me—I'm terrible*, try, *This wasn't the right fit, and that's okay*. Every rejection is an opportunity to grow, learn, and get closer to the people and opportunities that *are* meant for you.

It also helps to give yourself permission to feel the pain of rejection without letting it define you. Cry if you need to. Vent to a friend. Then dust yourself off and remind yourself that you're still amazing and someone else's opinion doesn't change that.

Focus on Pleasing Yourself First

This is *your* life. You're the one who has to live it, so you might as well make it a life you love. That means making choices based on what feels right for you—not what you think will earn you approval from others. When you prioritize your own happiness and values, you'll attract the people who genuinely appreciate you, and their opinions will carry a lot more weight than the haters' ever could.

Remember, you can't control what other people think about you. But you *can* control how much power you give their opinions. Let them judge. Let them not like you. It doesn't mean anything about your worth—because you, my friend, are a damn delight.

17

Be Impractical

There are words and phrases that as a life coach we're trained to listen for. If I meet you at a dinner party or even standing in line at a coffee shop and you casually say, "I've always wanted to...," you bet your butt I'll start salivating and asking more questions.

Have you always wanted to travel to Indonesia, write a book, or start an Etsy shop of knitted boots for cats? It doesn't matter what it is as long as it's mostly legal, I want to hear more about it and help you light a fire under your own ass to act on it.

Sometimes it's not necessarily an "I've always wanted to..." situation. One day I was on a call with my client Kelly. She had brought a topic to her coaching session—putting herself out there to promote her yoga business. Typically what's happening is that they're happy providing the product or service they offer, but they struggle to promote themselves, to tell people about their endeavor, and they stay stuck. So, that day with Kelly, we merrily rolled along in our conversation, and out of nowhere she says, "The thing that makes me the happiest is being around horses, but that's impractical."

I would be a terrible life coach if I told her to table that for later and circled her back to the topic at hand—her yoga business. These types of sentences do not in fact come out of nowhere. I believe they come blurting out when people feel safe, and the source is their intuition. Kelly knew I wouldn't laugh at her or agree it was a pipe dream, nor would I demand that she run out now and buy a horse to keep in her backyard. It came blurting out of her mouth because deep down Kelly knew that this was what her heart desired. Her soul longed to be around horses, to ride them, feed them, take care of them, and just be in their presence.

You know what brings me so much joy? When a client says those words. "The thing that makes me the happiest is ____, but that's impractical." When I hear those words, it's a "whomp there it is" moment. It's also juicy because the client immediately follows it up with some reason or excuse as to why they can't follow through with the thing that makes them happy, typically something like, "That's not possible, it's too hard, that's ridiculous, I'm embarrassed to say this, it's unattainable."

The truth is all dreams are impractical. If they weren't, they'd just be things on our to-do list.

What Happens If You Only Take the Practical Route?

The biggest obstacle to living your best life, to taking action on your dreams or even hobbies, is your inner critic—also known as plain old fear. More specifically, this is negative self-talk and you may be well aware and acquainted with this voice in your head. Countless self-help books, including my own, are dedicated to the topic, and I'm one to tell you that learning how to manage it is imperative and foundational to your happiness and fulfillment. I go in depth on the topic in *How to Stop Feeling Like Sh*t*, but I will tell you something important for you to understand about the pesky dream killer. Your inner critic has *one* goal. It has one primary expectation in its job description, and that's to keep you in your comfort zone.

It means well, it really does. Just like that sometimes passive-aggressive aunt who makes comments about how much you're on your phone when she visits, or that coworker who is privately keeping a log of how many minutes you're late each day—they swear they do it for your well-being, but in truth they're kind of assholes.

Your inner critic is trying to keep balance in your life but could really use some better communication strategies. Their only mode of communication is your thoughts, so it comes across as things like:

- *You'll look stupid if you try that.*
- *Look how much farther ahead she is than you.*
- *You're lazy, unattractive, old, (fill in the blank).*
- *You've wasted so much time in your life.*
- *It's not worth trying.*

And on and on. Your inner critic wants to keep you safe and from taking risks of any kind, so it constantly tells you how dangerous it is to put yourself out there. And hey, I'm not here to lie to you and tell you how not dangerous it is. When you step out of your comfort zone, when you do the impractical thing, eventually you will fail. Eventually you will make mistakes and be embarrassed or even ashamed. Eventually you will wonder why you ever took the risk in the first place and curse every self-help author you ever read. And I hope you do, because if that happens, I am surely doing my job of kicking you in the booty out of your comfort zone. May I remind you that you are not here to listen to your inner critic and do the practical, stay-in-the-box type of thing? You are not here to live a little life, totally safe and without any risk whatsoever.

Another clue that it may be time to ditch the practical life is if you have that sinking feeling, or even thought it, or said out loud the existential life question: *Is this all there is?*

Maybe it's in your job/career, your romantic relationship, what you do or don't do in your free time, or just your life in general. You could be at any age and have this feeling. Maybe you even reached your goals that you set years before and thought that achieving those goals would bring you all the fulfillment you ever needed. But you find yourself in that place people talk about when they're talking about a quarter-life or midlife or anytime-in-life crisis.

So, if you're asking, *Is this all there is?* dear reader, the answer is no, this isn't all there is. That question is a nudge for you from your built-in inner wisdom. It's pushing you toward more fulfillment and living your life according to your most burning desires. And many times, that wanting more will seem impractical, especially if you've settled for crumbs in your life. You'll look around and it may seem "good enough." It might be good, great even, but at the same time, you're missing something integral in terms of your happiness.

Speaking of midlife. As someone who's turned that corner, midlife can very much feel like a time when your life is trying to tell you something, whether it's a whisper or a flashing neon sign or a punch in the throat. The message can feel like, or in reality be, a breakdown in your life or just general discomfort. We know our youth is behind us. The second half of our life is here. At this point we typically have a clear understanding that our happiness and fulfillment are up to us. Life says, *We need to talk*. Those four words are scary coming from someone—or in this case, something—so substantial and important. So, when life tells you *We need to talk*, what is that talk? Is it that your romantic relationship has expired past the dealbreakers that you swore would really be dealbreakers? Is your career so incredibly unfulfilling that you long to run away to a foreign country and start over? Is your self-confidence nonexistent and you feel it's time to dig into it?

These are the questions I hope you give a damn about answering.

How to Be Positively Impractical

When it comes to striving toward or even plowing into living your best, most impractical life, you must learn how to trust yourself. When we're stuck listening to our inner critics, fear, the "safe" opinions of others, and living a more practical life rather than a kick-ass one, we find ourselves wishing we had more self-confidence. Self-trust and self-confidence are sisters, close as can be—not without their fights and pitfalls together, but sisters nonetheless.

When we want to do the fulfilling thing—for Kelly, it was spending more time with horses, but maybe for you it's wanting to start a side hustle, leave your relationship or start dating again, belly dancing, birding, or beatboxing—if it makes you feel alive, it's important. But when we categorize what we want as frivolous, a waste of time, or unimportant, there tend to be a few areas where we don't trust ourselves enough to follow through: not trusting we can overlook what people might say about our new endeavor; not trusting that we'll follow through with our goal; and not trusting it will work out.

Trust You Can Overlook What People Might Say About Your New Endeavor

Your mother-in-law, coworker, or that Facebook friend from high school whom you haven't seen in twenty years might all have their opinions about what you're doing: "Must be nice to have so much time on your hands!" or "Don't you work?"—any other passive-aggressive or snarky comments that make you question yourself for a second. On a conscious level, you might know that hurt people hurt people, and they're likely just envious that they don't have the guts to pursue their own dreams.

But . . . those comments still sting. They are never fun. And it might feel easier to not do the thing at all just to avoid them.

Instead, here's how to keep going, regardless of what anyone else says:

- **Anchor in your "why."** When those comments hit, remind yourself why you started. Your dream is worth more than their judgment.
- **Curate your support system.** Surround yourself with people who *get it*, who encourage you, and who remind you that you're on the right track.
- **Practice detachment.** Their words say more about *them* than they do about *you*. Let them have their opinions while you keep doing what's best for you.

At the end of the day, you don't need their approval. You only need your own. Keep going.

Embrace Your Many Interests and Trust Yourself to Follow Through

Raise your hand if you've ever had a million interests at once, your résumé bounces around like colors on a rainbow, and about every other month you're telling your friends about a *new* career path you're going to take. Many years ago, the author Barbara Sher coined the term *scanner* to describe people who have many passions and can't seem to pick just one.[1] This can also look a lot like ADHD.

If this is you, take a deep breath. There's nothing wrong with you. In fact, plenty of brilliant, successful people have followed winding paths. The key is not letting self-doubt stop you from exploring what makes you feel alive. If you've explored most of your interests and only followed through with one, guess what? You *win*. That's heaps better than never starting at all.

Here's how to embrace your curiosity *and* trust yourself in the process:

- **Reframe "flaky" as "curious."** You're not indecisive; you're multi-passionate. Own it and lean into the richness it brings to your life.
- **Look for patterns.** Even if your interests seem all over the place, there are usually common threads. Pay attention to what *really* excites you.
- **Redefine success.** Success doesn't mean sticking to one thing forever. It means pursuing what lights you up, even if that changes over time.

You don't have to choose just one passion forever. You just have to trust yourself enough to *keep going*.

Trust Yourself to Start, Even Without Guarantees

This might show up in a few ways. Maybe you don't trust that once you dive in, it'll be as fulfilling as you hoped. Perhaps you have bags upon bags of yarn collecting dust—your dream of making it big on Etsy with your crocheting business lost its sparkle when deadlines and demanding customers sucked the fun out of it. Now, with a new endeavor on the horizon, you're hesitant, wondering if this will end the same way.

Or maybe you don't trust that it will *work*. Especially if your big, exciting dream is meant to be more than a hobby—if you want it to be a *real* business. Your Magic 8 Ball said, "It is decidedly so," when you asked if you should go for it, but let's be honest—there is never, ever a guarantee.

Here's the truth: There's no promise you'll love it once you get started. You *might* change your mind. But starting something new is always vulnerable—that's just how it works. Instead of letting doubt stop you, here's how to build trust in yourself along the way:

- **Start small.** Set mini goals, micro habits, baby dreams—whatever you want to call them.

Keep them small and doable so you can build momentum.
- **Embrace the experiment.** Instead of thinking of this as an all-or-nothing commitment, treat it as an experiment. Give yourself permission to explore without pressure.
- **Track your wins.** Every step forward counts, even the tiny ones. Noticing your progress will build the self-trust and confidence to keep going.

You don't have to know *for sure* how it will all turn out. You just have to trust yourself enough to take the next step.

So, what is it that you'd do? What is that one "impractical" thing? Maybe it's researching. Or maybe you've researched your heart out and have realized one more Google search is just your procrastination and an effort to feel like you're doing something without actually doing anything. On this magical day, it's time to act. For my client Kelly, it was to call around to different horse stables to see if they needed volunteers. Maybe for you it's to start your DIY website or make an appointment for drag-racing lessons or fill out the forms to run for city council. At this point you understand there are risks; your inner critic makes that perfectly clear to you. You also understand this is heavily out of your comfort zone because it's that important to you. And most of all, you understand that you have one precious life and it was meant for living. Not for tiptoeing around, hoping the things you aspire to do will fall into your lap. Your life is for taking the time once in a while to run through it with your arms open, loving the shit out of it and loving the shit out of yourself.

Dealing with Your Inner Critic

Imagine a morning where you wake up and you have no concept of anyone else's opinion or judgment. No criticism to deal with, no sneaky eyes on your work. Not only that, but on this day, all of your thoughts are either positive or neutral. Not a hint of *You should be doing more* or *This will never work out*.

You get to just do what you had planned without the bombardment of doubt coming from you or anyone else.

The "how" in having this actually happen in your life is to first notice when you're doubting yourself, beating yourself up, or believing the lame excuses your inner critic comes up with. From there, get curious about those thoughts, asking yourself questions like:

- *Why do I think that won't work?*
- *What would I do if I didn't have that thought?*
- *What about this is so important that I'm hesitant to start?*
- *What might happen if I didn't have those thoughts that are holding me back?*

These questions are not so that you'll overthink it. Keep it simple and look at your fear, hesitation, and negativity around it with childlike wonder.

From there, try to create believable language that will put you in the direction to taking steps toward your goals and dreams.

- *There's always a chance this could work out.*
- *Even if it doesn't work out, the win is that I tried, and I'll be proud of that.*
- *I'm resourceful enough to figure out a way to make this work.*

When you're feeling the pull to take action on your Big Thing and feel hesitant, I invite you to take a moment to close your eyes and imagine the day I described above. You wake up and no one—not even you—has opinions, judgments, or criticisms about your dreams and ideas. An alternate universe where creating momentum on your Big Thing is just another to-do, like laundry or brushing your teeth. Not only is it no big deal but it's also necessary for your life.

Get Accountability

As you think about and plan the big leap that you're going to take, accountability is key for most people. This is one of the reasons people hire life coaches. A life coach will ask you all the right questions, remain curious, and help you get curious about your thoughts, beliefs, and actions. As the two of you strategize and plan together, your coach may also ask, "When will you do this, and how will I know?" A common and powerful question among life coaches, this often stumps our clients, many of whom are used to making big plans, feeling motivated for five minutes, then the inner critic kicks in and they abandon all plans and go back to watching cat videos on YouTube.

If "When will you do this, and how will I know?" makes you uncomfortable, that's a good thing. It means you're on to something big, it scares you, and it's important.

You don't have to hire a professional certified life coach to have accountability. You can ask a friend, but make sure this is intentional and well planned out. Not everyone is going to be pumped for you in your new endeavor. Or maybe they are, but if you don't tell them what you want your accountability to look like, they might not follow through.

***

My hope is that the words in this chapter make you think of the thing or things you deem impractical but that are still tapping on your heart, wanting to come to fruition.

You deserve to have the things that light you up become a real light in your life. It's your birthright to grab onto the feeling in your soul that is asking for more. This is your one, true life—to live like you give a damn is to run toward your desires.

18

Whatever You Think You Are Will Be Your Truth

Few things hold more power than the words that come out of your mouth—especially "I am." If you've ever stopped to listen to the way you speak about yourself, you might be shocked by how much of it is holding you back. We don't even realize it half the time because it's so automatic. We're out here saying things like "I'm such a mess," "I'm not good at this," or the classic "I'm just not that kind of person," like it's nothing. But guess what? Every time you say "I am," you're reinforcing an identity that sticks to you like glitter after a craft project, whether you want it to or not.

At first glance, this chapter's title, "Whatever You Think You Are Will Be Your Truth," might seem to contradict the titles of chapter 10, "How You Do One Thing Is Not How You Do Everything," and chapter 12, "Believe You Were Meant for and Deserve More." But personal growth isn't about rigid, black-and-white rules. It's about learning to hold multiple truths at once.

Yes, your mindset can shape your reality—your beliefs about yourself will probably influence your actions, confidence, and ultimately your results. But that doesn't mean you're stuck in one pattern across every area of your life.

Life is nuanced. You can struggle with confidence in one area while thriving in another.

And when I say, "Believe you were meant for and deserve more," I don't mean blind optimism. I mean consciously choosing to step into your potential even when your inner critic tells you otherwise. Your thoughts matter, but they are not the whole story. You get to challenge, shift, and rewrite them to align with the life you want.

Growth isn't about either-or thinking. It's about making space for all of it.

Here's the thing: You are the stories you tell yourself. The way you talk about yourself, the labels you casually slap on your identity, and the things you tell yourself you can or can't do—they all shape how you show up in the world. If those "I am" statements are negative, self-deprecating, or limiting, guess what happens? You stay stuck in an identity that isn't serving you. You half-ass the version of yourself you want to become because, deep down, your language is undermining your efforts.

Now, I get it—sometimes it feels easier to lean into self-deprecating humor or brush off compliments because we've been taught that modesty is a virtue. But let's be real here: Constantly apologizing, downplaying your strengths, and dismissing praise? That's not humility—that's self-sabotage. It's like you're saying, *I'm not worthy of taking up space.* And trust me, that's one of the biggest lies we tell ourselves.

When you're constantly downplaying your value, you're training your brain to believe that you're not capable of more. Every time you joke about how bad you are at something, or apologize for simply existing, you're reinforcing the idea that you're not enough. That's the real problem: These patterns of speaking and thinking have become so ingrained that you don't even notice how they're holding you back from the person you truly want to be.

What Happens If the Language You Use Is Shaping Your Reality?

Let's get real about how this language is impacting your life, because it's not just about words—it's about identity. The things you say about yourself aren't innocent comments—they shape the way you see yourself, the way you show up, and what you believe is possible for you.

Let's break it down. Imagine you're constantly telling yourself, *I'm not good at this*, whether it's in your career, your relationships, or even something like fitness. What happens? You start to believe it. You internalize that story and your brain looks for evidence to support it. You start to act in ways that reinforce that belief—maybe you don't try as hard, or you avoid situations where you could actually learn and grow. You've already decided that you're "not good" at it, so why bother, right?

Now apply that same logic to bigger things—like your ability to succeed in your career, find a fulfilling relationship, or chase your dreams. If you're constantly telling yourself, *I'm not that person*, you'll never allow yourself to become that person. You're cutting yourself off before you even give yourself a chance.

And we have to talk about self-deprecating humor. Look, I love a good laugh, but when you're constantly making yourself the punch line, you're sending a message to yourself (and to everyone else) that you don't take yourself seriously. It's like you're giving people permission to see you as less than. Sure, it might feel harmless in the moment, but over time, that self-deprecation chips away at your confidence and self-worth.

Then there's the whole unnecessary apologizing thing. How many times have you said sorry for something that didn't even require an apology? You bump into someone, you say, "Sorry." You voice your opinion in a meeting, you apologize. You take up space in a conversation, you feel the need to soften your words with an "I'm sorry, but . . ." It's almost as if you're apologizing for existing! And let me tell you, that needs to be a huge red flag *to yourself* that you're not standing in your full power. When you're always apologizing, you're essentially saying, *I don't have the right to be here* or *My voice doesn't matter*. And that's simply not true.

What's really happening here is that you're half-assing the identity you actually want. You've got one foot in the door of who you *could* be, but the other foot is still stuck in the muck of old beliefs and limiting language. The worst part? You don't even realize how much it's holding you back.

How to Change It—Tools and Strategies for Shifting Your Identity

So now that we've laid it all out on the table, it's time to get to work. The good news? You can absolutely change this. You have the power to rewrite the story you tell yourself and step into the identity you actually want to create. But—and here's the tough love—you've got to cut the shit when it comes to half-assing this process. You can't keep one foot in the door of your limiting beliefs while expecting to fully step into your greatness. So let's get started.

Watch Your "I Am" Statements

My client Olivia came to me feeling stuck in her career. She was a marketing manager who dreamed of starting her own business, but she constantly said things like, "I'm just not a risk-taker," or "I'm not entrepreneurial enough." Every time she said it, she was reinforcing a version of herself that couldn't grow into the business owner she wanted to be. Using Olivia as an example, let's break down what improving your self-talk in this area can look like.

> **Step 1: Notice the "I am" statements.** Start by paying attention to the stories you're telling yourself,

especially the "I am" statements. These are sneaky but powerful. Are you saying things like, "I'm not creative," "I'm bad with money," or "I'm too old to start over"? These phrases often go unnoticed, but they shape your reality.

Step 2: Flip the script in real time. When you catch yourself in one of these limiting statements, reframe it on the spot. Olivia went from "I'm not a risk-taker" to "I'm learning how to take calculated risks"; from "I'm not entrepreneurial enough" to "I'm building the skills I need to be a successful entrepreneur." It might feel awkward or untrue at first—like learning a new language—but keep practicing.

Olivia told me it felt like she was lying to herself, but over time, the new language began to stick. She started taking small steps toward her goal—creating a business plan, reaching out to potential mentors, and building her confidence. Today she's the proud owner of a thriving boutique agency, and it all started with changing the story she told herself.

Stop Unnecessary Apologizing

My friend Rachel was a classic over-apologizer. She'd say sorry for everything: if someone bumped into *her*, if she had a question in a meeting, even if she was running two minutes late to a Zoom call. It wasn't just a habit; it was a way she unconsciously minimized herself.

One day, Rachel vented to me about feeling overlooked at work. I asked her to start paying attention to how often she apologized and what she was apologizing for. It turned out her "sorries" were showing up everywhere, especially during team meetings. She'd preface her ideas with, "Sorry, but I was just thinking . . ." and people tended to gloss over her input.

I challenged her to replace "sorry" with more assertive language. Instead of "Sorry, but I was just thinking . . . ," she tried, "Here's an idea I'd like to share." Instead of apologizing for sending a follow-up email, she'd say, "Checking in on this."

It took some practice (and a sticky note on her computer that read "NO SORRY NEEDED!"), but Rachel started to notice a shift. People took her more seriously, and she felt more confident. A few months later, she was promoted, and she told me the best part was realizing she didn't have to apologize for showing up fully as herself.

Cut the Self-Deprecating Humor

Humor is great, but there's a fine line between laughing at yourself and tearing yourself down. If self-deprecating humor is your go-to, I want you to ask yourself, *What's the real reason I'm making myself the punch line? Is it because it feels safer to make fun of myself before someone else can? Is it because I don't want to come across as "too much" or "too confident"?*

Whatever the reason, it's time to work on it and cut it out. You don't need to make yourself smaller to fit in or be liked. Start practicing humor that lifts you up instead of tearing you down. And if you find yourself falling back into old habits, stop and remind yourself that you're worthy of taking up space without making yourself the joke.

Embrace Praise and Credit

Last but certainly not least, let's talk about accepting praise and credit. How many times have you deflected a compliment with a quick "Oh, it was nothing" or "I just got lucky"? You worked hard for your accomplishments, and you deserve to be recognized for them. The next time someone gives you a compliment, practice simply saying "Thank you" and letting those two words land. No deflecting, no downplaying—just receive it.

Let's all take notes from the character of Regina George in *Mean Girls*. Cady Heron says to her, "Your house is really nice!" And Regina replies, "I know, right?"[1]

It might feel uncomfortable at first, but the more you do it, the more you'll start to believe that you're worthy of praise and credit. And guess what? You *are*.

***

At the end of the day, the way you talk about yourself has the power to shape your reality. If you want to step into your full power and create the identity you truly desire, it starts with cutting the limiting language and half-assed beliefs that have been holding you back. Watch your "I am" statements, stop apologizing for existing, cut way back on the self-deprecation, and embrace your worth. You're not here to play small—you're here to live a life that's aligned with the most outstanding version of yourself. You're here to live like you give a damn.

And remember: The words you use about yourself aren't just words—they're declarations of who you are and who you're becoming. So choose them wisely, and watch how everything around you starts to shift.

19

The Big-Wig Boss of Personal Development: Purpose

Searching the internet for "how to find my purpose" will yield 7.6 billion hits. After working in the personal growth space for nearly twenty years, I can tell you this is one of the most common questions I get from people.

Of course, we want to know our purpose—it's part of being human. It's the universal question of "How can I make sure my life matters?" which then translates to "How can I make sure that *I* matter?" Lucky for us, our language has distilled these two huge existential questions into one word that is supposed to be the answer to those questions and the solution to all our woes. A word that many people utter with such reverence, as if saying it will conjure the most important thing we'll ever encounter in our lives: *purpose*.

When Emily came to me for coaching, she was tangled up in this very question. After her fortieth birthday, she felt an overwhelming sense of failure for not having "figured out her purpose" yet. She told me, "It feels like everyone else has a map and I'm just wandering around lost." Emily was successful in her career, had a rich social life, and was deeply caring toward her family, but none of it felt like *enough*.

She described her fear of "wasting" her life if she didn't discover her purpose soon.

As we dug into this, I asked Emily a question that caught her off guard: "What if there's no singular purpose for you to find?" Her reaction was immediate. "But then what's the point of all of this?" she asked, gesturing broadly. "How do I know if I'm doing it right?"

The truth is, none of us know for sure what our purpose is or anyone else's. It's all made up—all of it. Of course, we can have that feeling, that intuitive hit that something is important and special to us, but the bottom line is no one really knows for sure.

Here's the good news: We're going to unpack this topic together. If you've ever felt stuck, anxious, or unsure about what purpose even means, you're not alone—and there's a way forward.

What Happens If You Put Too Much Focus on Purpose?

The obsession around your purpose can leave you feeling bad about yourself—or worse, panicked. Have you ever met or do you know of someone who seems like they have *all* their shit together? More specifically, they have that job or hobby that seems like it's both fulfilling to them and maybe even helps others? They may even describe it as "their purpose," passionately describing their fulfillment and sense of contentment. Meanwhile, you're just over here on Pinterest looking for "easy weeknight dinners" and wondering if not burning dinner counts as a purpose. This person's focus can then make *you* feel like you're failing at life, scrambling to find your life purpose.

The first thing I'd like you to do around this topic is to define what that word *purpose* conjures up for you. Some people immediately know and may feel triggered by it; other people, not so much. So, what does "purpose" mean to you? Is it loaded, feeling somewhat weighted? Or something else?

As I mentioned, when we're talking about purpose, what we're usually looking for is the knowledge that our life matters. That what we're putting out into the world with our connections, ideas, and actions makes a difference to someone—anyone—and the collective. (And make no mistake, if you've ever made someone laugh so hard they snorted, that's making a difference.) We're looking for a meaningful life.

So, what does it mean to live a fulfilling, meaningful life? One that makes us feel like we're living our purpose? Let's get into it.

How to Let Go of the Pressure of Purpose (. . . and How to Possibly Find It)

When we're diving into the idea of life purpose, it's natural to hit some obstacles along the way because it's such a vast topic. Let's explore the four big ones: not knowing what purpose means to you, being unclear about what truly matters in your life, defining your values, and grappling with your very human need for certainty. A practice follows unpacking these.

Obstacle 1: Defining Purpose

The first obstacle is one I've already hinted at: If you had to define *purpose*, what would you say it means? Take a moment with this. Once you have an answer, ask yourself, *How does that definition make me feel?*

If your reaction includes heavy or difficult emotions like confusion, sadness, or even frustration, this is your cue to get curious. These emotions aren't roadblocks; they're signposts. Ask yourself why those feelings are coming up or what is behind or underneath the emotions. Is it because of pressure you've put on yourself? Expectations from others or society? Or perhaps a fear of getting it wrong? Spend some time unpacking those feelings before moving forward.

If, on the other hand, your definition of purpose feels exciting, hopeful, or positive, lean into that energy as we continue. These emotions might signal that you're already connecting with something meaningful. Use that as your foundation for what comes next.

Obstacle 2: What If You Don't Need "a" Purpose?

Here's a game-changer: What if you don't actually need a life purpose? What if tomorrow morning you woke up and the pressure to define your life by a single purpose was lifted? How would that feel? Like unbuttoning a pair of jeans after Thanksgiving dinner, right? Instant relief.

Focus on the word *a*. So often we're conditioned to believe that purpose must be one grand, monumental thing. But what if it's not? What if your purpose is a collection of smaller, equally important things—a patchwork of experiences, contributions, and joys? A collection of connections, your journey of healing, or coming home to yourself as you age? Imagine how freeing that could be. It's like realizing you don't have to pick just one thing off the menu at your favorite restaurant—life's too short not to enjoy the whole menu. Maybe you'd feel less panicked, more open to exploring, and more accepting of the idea that your purpose might evolve over time.

If the idea of having no purpose at all feels like the right fit for you, that's valid. What might that openness create in your life? Perhaps more space to explore, more freedom to simply be, or more joy in the present moment.

Obstacle 3: Values as a Compass

One of the best ways to create meaning in your life—whether or not you're aiming to define a purpose—is by doing values work. Your values are the guiding principles that shape how you want to live, who you want to be, and what makes life meaningful for you.

Consider values like kindness, courage, creativity, or growth. Now think about what makes your life feel significant. Is it serving others? Embracing adventure? Deeply connecting with people, whether they're loved ones or strangers? If you close your eyes and picture yourself in scenarios that embody these values, do you feel like your life has meaning? Does it feel like your cup of life is full?

Here's another way to approach this: Reflect on what brings you joy. For example, as I write this chapter, I'm sitting in a coffee shop. A woman a few tables away bursts out laughing while looking at her phone. I have no idea what made her laugh, but witnessing her joy fills me up. It feels like a privilege to share in that moment, even from afar.

What are your moments like that? Is it practicing kindness? Honoring your hobbies? Volunteering for causes close to your heart? Knowing what fills you with joy is just the first step. The next, equally important step is to pause and savor it. Feel the joy, let it settle, and take a moment to be grateful for it. That joy—that presence—could be your life's purpose right there.

Obstacle 4: Our Need for Certainty

Finally, let's talk about the need for certainty. We humans love patterns, templates, and answers. Throw in a Magic 8 Ball that tells us exactly what we want to hear, and we're happy as a clam. Certainty feels safe. But emotions, which are at the heart of this work, are unpredictable. They're messy. And that can leave us feeling vulnerable—sometimes to the point where we avoid them altogether.

The truth is, exploring your purpose is emotional work. It's about stepping into the unknown and being okay with not having all the answers. How can you start building that muscle? One way is by practicing curiosity over judgment. When uncertainty comes up, instead of trying to fix it or make it go away, ask yourself, *What's here for me to learn?*

You can also create small, safe experiments to get comfortable with the unknown. For example, try something new without knowing how it will turn out—take a dance class, start a creative project, or volunteer for something outside your comfort zone. As you do, notice how it feels to embrace the uncertainty. That's where growth lives.

The key takeaway here is that you don't need to have everything figured out. In fact, your purpose might be less about finding answers and more about learning to live fully in the questions.

Getting back to my client Emily. Together we explored her assumptions about purpose. For Emily, the word felt heavy, like an invisible deadline she'd already missed. But as she reflected on what truly mattered to her—her values of connection, creativity, and growth—she started to see things differently. Purpose wasn't some singular, magical thing she had to unearth; it was in the way she chose to show up every day.

Emily came to realize that her life already *mattered*—to her friends, her family, her coworkers, and even to herself. She began to lean into her values more intentionally, finding joy in the little things: reconnecting with an old friend, painting for the first time in years, and volunteering for a cause she cared about. She discovered that these moments made her life feel full of meaning.

By the end of our work together, Emily no longer felt panicked about purpose. Instead, she felt free. Her purpose wasn't about one grand answer but a series of small, meaningful choices that brought her closer to the life she wanted to live.

What if you could lean into the perspective that your life can have meaning if you choose to accept that it can be full of a series of small but significant experiences? That living your values, prioritizing your connections with others, and focusing on your personal growth could very well be the thing that is your life purpose?

20

You're Not Doing Life Wrong

Years ago, I had a listener Q&A segment on my podcast. People would write in with questions pertaining to their personal growth and ask for advice. Sara emailed in with the following question:

> I beat myself up over the fact that I can't seem to get anything right! I feel dumb saying that, I live a relatively nice life, it's not like I'm alone and destitute or anything. I feel like I've always been capable of so much more and somehow am too defective to make it work. I screwed up college so bad I never graduated. I've had opportunities pass me by because I either start and never finish or don't bother because I know I'll f*** it up. Now here I am staring forty in the face and what am I? Like, shouldn't I know by now? I get in my head and make great plans and goals and dreams and I just can't get out of my own way to make it work. I don't think I'm doing life right.

Sara's feelings aren't uncommon. Many people, especially as they make their way through their thirties and into their forties and beyond, feel life's pressures and responsibilities stacking up. The expectations pile up, and then I hear the prevailing sentiment of feeling like they're screwing up and "doing life wrong."

I think about myself circa 2006. There I was, dumped by my husband for another woman. I had quit my job for a man I was deeply invested in, only to later realize he was struggling with addiction. I had pushed away all of my friends for my new boyfriend. I was also broke, in debt, and had to move in with my older sister. (She *had* what I deemed "her shit together"—she was married and had a good job, kids, a mortgage, all the things I didn't have.) I felt like everything was quickly falling apart in my life. Some might even say I was doing life wrong and that I needed to get myself together. Hell, I said that to myself. Even in the midst of all that chaos, when I eventually woke up and *knew* I was making bad choices, when I *knew* I needed to change . . . I chose to stay. I chose to keep living like I was living, for months.

I had my thirty-first birthday during that period of time in my life. Most, if not all, of my friends were getting on with their lives, getting married, building careers, buying homes, having children—most of the things we're told make us "successful" both in the eyes of ourselves and others. However, I was going backward on this track, careening toward a life I never anticipated, one that very much made me feel like I was doing it all wrong.

What Happens If You Feel Like You're "Doing Life Wrong"?

Doing life "right" is one of the biggest and most universal pressures we face in our culture. To feel that your life isn't on the "right track" can bring on discomfort at best and crushing shame at worst. Not only does our culture make up markers and mileposts for what "success" is but commonly our families do as well. Not to mention how easy it is to fall into the comparison trap. We look at others' lives—our friends, our family, people we see online—and measure ourselves against their "success," only to come up short every time. It's enough to make us feel like we'll never climb out of the hole we're convinced we're in.

This comparison and positioning only keeps us further stuck. Whenever we're in a spiral or pattern of negative thinking, those thoughts breed among themselves, furthering more negative thoughts. From there, those thoughts heavily impact how we feel about ourselves, and that tends to dictate our behavior. We essentially end up trying tirelessly to dig ourselves out of a hole while throwing more dirt in.

Over my near two decades of working with clients on their lives, I can tell you I've had many, many conversations with people about how they want their lives to change. After they tell me their goals, they then let their guard down about how stressed they are because they aren't far enough along, they're not where they "should" be, and they feel like they're doing life wrong. This stress is very real, so let's dig in so this doesn't happen to you.

How to Let Go of Feeling Like You're "Doing Life Wrong"

The concept of "doing life right" is a giant, shimmering red flag of perfectionism and too-high expectations. These unrealistic assumptions about where you think you "should" be need to be addressed.

Get out a piece of paper or your favorite note-taking app and make a list, asking yourself, *What do I make up "having your shit together" to mean?* Write it all down. (Notice I say what you "make up." This is intentional because it's all made up.) Where do you think someone like you should be at this point in their life? In response to Sara's question, I specifically asked her what she thought a woman who's about to turn forty should have accomplished by now. Get as specific as possible. Don't hold back here; really list out anything and everything you can think of.

On this list can be both tangible and intangible things. For example, maybe you make up that, at this point in your life, you should have a particular job title and a certain salary. In addition, you expected yourself to feel confident and stop being such a people pleaser, yet you still find yourself lacking self-confidence and saying yes to things you don't want to, which coincidentally impacts your professional goals.

You may start making this list and quickly realize your expectations are unrealistic and then think you're done with the exercise. No, ma'am. Keep going. These thoughts and beliefs are deeply rooted, and we need to yank out these roots and inspect them. Let's keep going.

Gray Area, Seasons, Ebb and Flow, and Pain Tolerance

In her question, Sara says, "I get in my head and make great plans and goals and dreams, and I just can't get out of my own way to make it work." Sara might be making up these grand plans, goals, and dreams, and then when it comes to taking action, it's all just too much. Most of the smart, high-achieving women I attract in my community think this way. It's all or nothing: Either I take on the world, or I'm nothing. Either I am crazy successful, or I'm a lazy piece of shit. There is no in-between.

The truth is, as I talked about in chapter 10, life isn't black or white. If you make it that way, you'll always—and I mean always—fail, feel like an epic loser, and worry you'll end up being known as "the town eccentric" in your community. Look for the gray area, the tiny steps of action or learning, and even the times you've been successful and fallen backward. Those successes still count, and I guarantee you have many of them that you're not giving yourself credit for.

I, too, am a recovering all-or-nothing kind of girl, so I know the middle ground, and failing, and getting back up are *hard*.

But you have to make tiny turtle steps in order to grow and to go after what you want.

In addition to looking out for your all-or-nothing thinking, look for where you expect life to be linear. It never, ever is. Just like the moon, the tides, and a woman's menstrual cycle, life has seasons. Sometimes life is full of blooms and new life, and sometimes we encounter cold and we face darkness. Do some "winters" feel long and treacherous? Yes, but I assure you, your "spring" is right around the corner.

Getting to where your goals and the need to change are for you and no one else is a magical place to be, and an important one, but it's not where you'll begin to take action. You'll only take consistent action when staying where you are hurts more than changing. When complaining that you're "doing life wrong" pains you more than going after those opportunities you've been passing up or creating new opportunities for yourself. I believe all of us have a pain tolerance, and once we reach our threshold, something breaks loose and we start to move. Only you know where that is for you. Maybe you'll have a life-changing moment like I did. Maybe you just get uncomfortable like Sara. Or maybe you'll just wake up one day and decide what the most important thing is to come next for you.

PERSONAL MANIFESTO

One of my favorite exercises when it comes to taking inventory of what's actually important to you (and only you) is to create your own manifesto. A manifesto is your personal North Star—a declaration of what lights you up, what you believe, and what you stand for. It's part compass, part permission slip to live life on your terms. It's not rigid or perfect; it evolves as you do. When you feel stuck or lost, it's your reminder of who you are and what truly matters to you.

When you finish the sentences below, you can make art out of it or share it with others. Revisit your manifesto on a regular basis. Just like you do, just like your goals do, and just like your life does, your manifesto will change over time.

Get out a piece of paper and finish the following sentences:

- I believe ...
- I stand for ...
- I am most passionate about ...
- I am on this planet to ...
- I was born in this time and space so that I can ...
- I will love myself by ...
- I will honor my life by ...
- I have the courage to ...
- I will take action on ...
- The status quo I want to disrupt is ...
- What I want to create more is ...
- What matters to me right now is ...
- What I know for sure is ...

Your Turn

Now that you've created your manifesto, take a moment to sit with it. Read it out loud. Let the words sink in. Does it feel true? Does it feel empowering? Does it give you that little jolt of energy or a sense of calm clarity? If not, that's okay. Sometimes it takes revisiting and tweaking. What's important is that these words come from you, not from the expectations of others or the "shoulds" that have taken root in your mind.

This is your declaration of what matters, what drives you, and what you're here to do. It's not set in stone; it will evolve just as you do, but it's a beautiful starting point. And when you're in a moment of self-doubt or feel like you're "doing life wrong," come back to this. It's your anchor.

If you take away anything from this chapter, let it be this: There is no singular, universal, or perfect way to "do life." Such an idea only keeps you stuck, spinning in a cycle of comparison and self-judgment. Your path is yours, and it doesn't have to look like anyone else's.

Sara's story, my story, and probably parts of your story are all proof that life isn't linear. It's messy, unpredictable, and full of seasons. Some are bright and abundant, and others are dark and cold. But each one shapes who we are and helps us find our own version of success, fulfillment, and joy.

Your next step is simple but powerful: Start small. Challenge your expectations. Create your manifesto. Reflect on your seasons and trust that you are capable of navigating them. And remember, you're not doing life wrong—you're just doing it your way: the way you live like you give a damn.

21

Redefine Winning

When you think of "winning," what comes to mind? For many of us, winning equals success—it's all about the big, flashy, high-stakes moments. The gold medal, the dream career, the Instagram-worthy life. It's about being on top, being the best, and let's be honest, often it's about competing with everyone around us. But winning can also show up in quieter ways—achieving at all costs, not necessarily for the spotlight but for the satisfaction of checking every box, meeting every goal, or proving something to yourself or others.

We've been conditioned to see winning—and therefore success—in a very narrow way: You either succeed by society's standards or you don't. You either meet all the expectations that have been set for you or you fall short. And let's not forget the constant pressure to "win" at life in every possible area. You may feel you've got to be crushing it at work, in your relationships, with your health, with your finances—oh, and you better be smiling while you're doing it. Exhausting, right? No wonder so many of us feel like we're not "winning." We're trying to play a game that's rigged against us.

The problem with this traditional view of success is that it's based on external metrics. It's about how you stack up against others, not how you feel about yourself. It's about what society, social media, your family, or even your inner critic expects from you rather than what truly matters to you right now. When we measure ourselves by these standards, we often come up short. We feel like we're failing, even if we're doing the best we can with what we have.

If you're going to live like you give a damn, self-confidence needs to be part of the equation. And real self-confidence doesn't come from just "winning" or getting everything right. It comes from experience—all kinds of experience. Not just the successes but also the missteps, the flops, and the times we thought we couldn't bounce back but did. Confidence is built in the doing, not in the perfect outcome. In this chapter, we're going to talk about what it means to redefine success and why your experience—especially the messy, imperfect parts—matters more than any external scoreboard.

There's real wisdom in pausing to reflect before charging full speed ahead. Who says success or winning is only about being the best, the most, or the fastest? Why do we think we're only "winning" when we're overachieving in every aspect of life? The truth is, you don't have to buy into that story. It's not yours. It's time to rewrite it.

What Happens If the Pressure to "Win" Is Sucking the Joy Out of Your Journey?

The impact of chasing this traditional idea of winning is no joke. When you're constantly measuring yourself by someone else's standards, it's like trying to hit a moving target. You're always falling short, always feeling like you're behind, and always stressed about what you *should* be doing. You end up stuck in a cycle of striving for more but never quite feeling like you've done enough.

One of the biggest ways this shows up is in the way we set our goals. Think about it: How often have you set a goal that was based on what you thought you *should* be doing rather than what you actually wanted? Maybe it was climbing the corporate ladder because that's what success looks like in your industry. Maybe it was getting into the best shape of your life because society equates fitness and the shape of our bodies with worthiness. Maybe it was becoming the perfect partner or parent because that's what everyone around you seems to be doing.

When we set our goals based on what we think success looks like to others, we lose sight of what actually matters to us. We end up pursuing goals that don't align with our values. Then we wonder why we feel so unfulfilled even when we achieve them. It's like running a race you don't even want to be in, crossing the finish line and realizing it didn't matter after all.

Let's not forget about the pressure that comes with trying to succeed at everything all the time. It's suffocating. You're so focused on the end result—on the "win"—that you forget to take in the process. You become obsessed with productivity, with ticking things off your to-do list, with proving your worth through achievement. You start to see rest, self-care, and anything that isn't directly related to winning as a waste of time.

But here's the truth: Constantly chasing this idea of succeeding/winning is draining your confidence and your joy. You're setting yourself up for disappointment and possibly burnout because the bar is always moving. You're so busy trying to be everything to everyone that you forget to live your life. And what happens when you inevitably fall short? You go full-on self-critique mode, hand yourself a participation trophy for failure, and your confidence ghosts you like a potential date on a dating app. It's a vicious cycle, and it's one that needs to end.

How to Change It—Redefine What Winning Looks Like for You

So now that we've called out the problem, let's talk about how to change it. Here's the good news: You get to define what winning, and thus success, looks like for you. You don't have to play by anyone else's rules. You get to set the standards, decide what matters, and define success on your own terms. So let's dig into how to do that.

Establish What's Actually Important to You

The first step to redefining winning is to get clear on what's truly important to you. We talked about values in chapter 19, and I mention them often because (a) what's important to you is important to you, period, end of story; and (b) this is a hill I will die on. Not to mention, your values are pivotal in living like you give a damn.

This is not what your parents, your boss, or society tells you should be important but what really matters to *you*. Take a look at your life and ask yourself, *Are my goals aligned with my values?*

If you're not sure, start by identifying your core values. These are the things that matter most to you—the guiding principles that make you feel like you're living authentically. Maybe it's connection, creativity, freedom, adventure, or personal growth. Whatever your values are, they should be at the heart of how you define winning.

Once you've got a sense of what's important to you, take a good look at your current goals. Are they aligned with those values? If not, it's time to reassess. Because here's the thing: If you're chasing goals that don't align with your values, you're never going to feel like you're winning and self-confidence will feel elusive, no matter how much you achieve.

Set Realistic and Compassionate Goals

Now that you've identified your values and started to realign your goals, it's time to talk about setting yourself up for success. And by success I don't mean hitting some arbitrary milestone.

I mean setting goals that are realistic, compassionate, and designed to build your confidence.

Here's where most of us get it wrong. We set goals that are so high, so out of reach, that we're practically guaranteeing our own failure. We think that if we just push harder, do more, or grind through the exhaustion, we'll finally get there. But that's not how it works. When you set impossible goals, you're setting yourself up to feel like a failure, even if you've made progress.

Instead, focus on small, achievable steps that move you closer to where you want to be. And let's be real: Some days, winning doesn't mean crushing it; it means doing the bare minimum to keep things moving while also taking care of yourself. Because survival days count too. In fact, sometimes the biggest win is giving yourself the grace to slow down, rest, and acknowledge that you're human—not a machine—and that you're doing your best.

So, ask yourself, *What's possible for one human to do today?* Not a superhuman. Not a robot. A real, living, breathing human with needs, emotions, *lots* of responsibilities, and limitations. That's where you set the bar. And when you hit those small, realistic goals, celebrate them. Because every small step forward—whether it's a leap or a crawl—is a win.

Question What Winning Really Means

Let's get real about where your definition of winning comes from. So many of us are walking around with someone else's idea of success rattling around in our heads, and we don't even realize it. Maybe it's the voice of society telling you that you need to be constantly productive. Maybe it's the voice of your parents telling you that a certain career path is the only way to succeed. Maybe it's the voice of your past self, who had different priorities and expectations fifteen years ago.

Whatever it is, it's time to question it. Use the prompts below to help you dig deeper and start creating a version of success that's actually yours. Get out a piece of paper or your favorite note-taking app and journal on the following questions.

- Whose idea of winning or success have I been chasing?
- Do I actually believe in this version of success or have I just adopted it without question?
- Does this definition of winning make sense for the life I want to live?
- Does it align with my values, my goals, and my well-being?
- What does *my* version of success look and feel like right now?

If your current definition of success doesn't align with your life, values, or truth, it's okay to let it go. You don't have to prove anything to anyone. Focus on your version of success being living a life that feels fulfilling, aligned, and true to who you are.

Take Incremental Steps Toward Your Version of Winning

Once you've redefined winning for yourself, the next step is to start moving toward it. And guess what? You don't have to overhaul your entire life in one dramatic gesture. In fact, real, lasting change happens in small, incremental steps.

Here's the magic of incremental progress: It builds confidence. When you take small, manageable steps toward your goals, you're setting yourself up for success. Each step forward, no matter how small, reinforces the belief that you can do this. You're proving to yourself, little by little, that you're capable, that you're winning, and that you're on the right track.

So, what's one small thing you can do today to move closer to your new definition of winning? Maybe it's saying no to something that doesn't align with your values. Maybe it's setting a small boundary that honors your well-being. Maybe it's celebrating the fact that you made it through the day without burning out. Whatever it is, honor it. Celebrate it. And trust that those small steps will add up to big, meaningful wins over time.

Give Yourself Grace

Finally, let's talk about grace. Because here's the truth: You're not going to feel like you're "winning" every day. There will be times when you fall short, when things don't go as planned, and when you wonder if you're doing enough. And that's okay. In fact, it's normal. You're human, not a productivity robot—or Beyoncé (and even she has twenty-four hours in a day).

This is where grace comes in. Give yourself permission to be imperfect, to rest, to fail, and to get back up again. Some days, winning looks like crushing your to-do list; other days, it's just remembering where you left your phone. Winning isn't about being flawless or having it all together all the time—it's about learning, evolving, and finding joy in the journey. So when you slip up, when you feel like you're not doing enough, remember: You're still winning. Because real winning is about self-compassion, resilience, and embracing the messiness of life—like the forgotten laundry in the washer you'll rewash tomorrow.

When you redefine winning on your terms, you stop measuring yourself by someone else's standards and start living in alignment with your values. You stop chasing after the elusive "perfect" life and instead celebrate the small, meaningful steps you're taking to become the best version of yourself.

So, here's the final truth: You're already winning. You are worthy, capable, and enough exactly as you are. The moment you let go of the pressure to fit into a narrow, external definition of success is the moment you start to realize that winning has always been about embracing your own path, one step at a time.

Now go ahead—redefine what winning means for you, and celebrate every little victory along the way.

22

Check Your Expectations

If you're like most women, expectations are a constant companion. You've been surrounded by them your whole life—whether they've come from society, family, your job, or even from within. We're told to aim high, strive for more, and keep pushing forward. And let's be honest: That drive can be a good thing. Setting goals and having standards based on our version of excellence helps us achieve success and live meaningful lives.

But here's the thing: There's a fine line between having high standards and creating an unachievable list of expectations for yourself. When we start stacking our plates too high—juggling work, home, relationships, health, hobbies, self-care, and a hundred other things—it's easy to spiral into overwhelm. At some point, it's like trying to balance a buffet on a paper plate at a barbecue—something's bound to slide off. Unrealistic expectations thrive in these moments. They whisper, *You should do more. You should handle this. You should be better.*

Let me paint the picture: You set out to tackle your day. Maybe it's a major work project, a personal event like planning a birthday party, or simply managing your endless to-do list. At first you feel excited and determined. But as the expectations you've placed on yourself grow, that determination starts to shift. Suddenly you're thinking some version of, *If I don't accomplish every single thing perfectly, it's not enough. I'm not enough.*

Sound familiar? That's not just ambition talking. That's the weight of expectations that have tipped from motivating to debilitating. Before you know it, you're hobbling around like someone trying to carry a week's worth of groceries in one trip—keys in your mouth, a bag slipping off your shoulder, and that one rogue orange making a break for it down the driveway.

Here's where the problem lies: Striving for excellence isn't the issue. The issue arises when we're chasing expectations so high, so numerous, or so unrealistic that they set us up for failure, burnout, and the sudden urge to google "How to clone myself immediately." We're no longer pursuing what's important to *us*. Instead, we're operating under a relentless barrage of "should." And let's be clear, those "shoulds" often aren't even ours. They're handed down from societal norms, family pressures, or that inner critic telling us we need to keep up with everyone else.

The reality is that these towering expectations don't lead to fulfillment. They are a direct line to burnout. They're a trap that leaves us running in circles, chasing some impossible idea of "doing it all" without ever stopping to ask if it's worth the cost.

What Happens If the Weight of Too-High Expectations Is Impacting Your Life?

Now let's dig into the ripple effects of carrying these overwhelming expectations. Spoiler alert: They're not just a "little quirk" of your personality—they're taking a toll on your life in significant ways.

First off, let's talk exhaustion. When your list of expectations looks more like a scroll, you're constantly running on empty, trying to keep up. You're overcommitting, overplanning, and overthinking. No matter how much you do, it feels like it's never enough. That's because there's always another task to complete, another standard to meet, another goal to crush.

It's not just your body that feels it—it's your mind and emotions too. Unrealistic expectations bring their buddy, self-doubt, to the party. When you inevitably can't meet every standard, your inner critic chimes in: *Why couldn't you handle that? You're letting everyone down.* Cue the guilt and shame spiral. This isn't about being lazy or unmotivated; it's about being human. Humans have limits, and when you're constantly pushing past them, it chips away at your confidence and self-worth.

But the impact doesn't stop there. These towering expectations can paralyze you. You might hesitate to take on new challenges because you're afraid you won't measure up. You might avoid trying something new because you think, *If I can't do it perfectly, why bother at all?* Instead of living boldly and embracing life's messy, imperfect moments, you end up stuck in a loop of overthinking and underacting.

And let's be real about how this spills into relationships. When you're holding yourself to impossible standards, it's easy to start projecting them onto others. You might expect your partner to anticipate your every need, your friends to never make mistakes, or your coworkers or team to meet every deadline flawlessly. When people inevitably fall short of these sky-high standards, it can lead to frustration, resentment, and distance.

The bottom line? Unrealistic expectations aren't just inconvenient. They're harmful. They drain your energy, steal your joy (and your soul), and keep you stuck in a cycle of stress and self-doubt. But here's the good news: You *can* shift the narrative. You can learn to differentiate between what truly matters and what's just noise. And you can free yourself from the weight of those expectations to create a life that feels fulfilling and achievable.

How to Master Expectation Management

So, how do we break free from this perfectionism trap? How do we reclaim our lives from the weight of impossible expectations? It all comes down to something I like to call "expectation management," which can be distilled into five principles. It's about stripping down the unrealistic standards your inner critic has set for you and consciously choosing expectations that align with who you are and what's humanly possible.

Identify the Source of Your Expectations

The first stage in managing your expectations is getting clear on where they're coming from. Are they truly yours or are they the product of societal pressures, family dynamics, or that pesky inner critic? Are they based in perfectionism, and if so, where does that come from? Take a moment to reflect on the expectations you've set for yourself in different areas of your life—work, relationships, health, personal growth.

Ask yourself, *Whose voice is setting this expectation? Is it my own or is it someone else's? Have I internalized external pressures that don't actually align with my values and the person I want to become?* By bringing awareness to the source of your expectations, you can start to separate the ones that serve you from the ones that are sabotaging you and keeping you stuck.

Embrace Realistic Expectations

Once you've identified the unrealistic expectations you've been carrying, it's time to start setting realistic ones. This doesn't mean lowering your standards or giving up on excellence. It means being kind to yourself and acknowledging that you're a human being, not a robot. You have limits, and that's okay.

So, what does setting realistic expectations look like? It's about checking in with what's actually possible for you in a given moment. It's about taking into account your energy levels, your time constraints, and your mental and emotional bandwidth. Instead of expecting yourself to do everything flawlessly all at once, focus on doing a few things well—and give yourself grace when things don't go as planned.

Remember, excellence is still on the table, but it's excellence that's achievable and sustainable—not perfectionism that's suffocating. Set goals that stretch you but don't stress and break you.

Differentiate Between Excellence and Perfectionism

Here's a little secret: Excellence and perfectionism are not the same thing. Excellence is about doing your best with what you've got, striving for growth, and learning from your mistakes. It's about what's important to you and only you. Perfectionism, on the other hand, is about fear. It's about trying to prove to other people (and that's an important distinction) your worth by being flawless, which is a losing game because—and you know this—flawless doesn't exist.

So, how do you know if you're aiming for excellence or falling into perfectionism? Excellence feels challenging but empowering. It's about growth, not validation. Excellence is about your values and what's important to *you*.

Perfectionism, on the other hand, feels restrictive and anxiety-inducing. It's about trying to avoid criticism or judgment by others rather than genuinely improving yourself. Perfectionism is about the story you make up around what others expect from you.

Get out your favorite journal or note-taking app, and use the prompts below to check in with yourself and recalibrate when needed:

- Am I striving for growth or am I trying to avoid failure?
- Is this about what I want or what I think others want from me?
- Is this connected to my values or is it fueled by fear of judgment?
- Does this feel empowering and aligned or stressful and constricting?

If your answers lean toward fear, avoidance, or outside validation, it's time to pause and recalibrate. Excellence is about honoring your own path, not chasing someone else's impossible standard.

Give Yourself Permission to Be Human

One of the most powerful things you can do to manage your expectations is to give yourself permission to be human. Newsflash: You're allowed to make mistakes. You're allowed to have bad days. You're allowed to be imperfect. In fact, embracing your imperfections is one of the keys to living a more joyful, authentic life.

So the next time your inner critic starts berating you for not meeting some impossible standard, pause and remind yourself, *I am enough as I am, flaws and all*. It's not about letting yourself off the hook—it's about showing yourself the same kindness and grace you'd show to a friend.

Align Your Expectations with Your Integrity

Finally, one of the most important aspects of expectation management is making sure your expectations are in alignment with your personal integrity. What do I mean by that? Your expectations should reflect your values and what's truly important to you—not what society, your nosy neighbor who comments on your lawn, or a random Instagram influencer with suspiciously perfect hair tells you should be important.

For example, if you value personal growth and creativity, then set goals that push you to grow and express yourself creatively. But don't set goals based on external validation or societal pressures if they don't resonate with you. When your expectations align with your integrity, you'll find that you're more motivated, more resilient, and more fulfilled.

At the end of the day, expectation management is about giving yourself the freedom to be human, the grace to be imperfect, and the courage to aim for excellence without falling into perfectionism. You get to decide what success looks like for you, and you get to set the terms for how you're going to achieve it.

Expectations aren't inherently bad, but they become harmful when they're unrealistic, misaligned with our values, or driven by perfectionism. By stripping away the unrealistic standards of your inner critic and embracing expectations that are in alignment with who you are, you can start living a life that feels empowered, fulfilled, and truly yours.

So, my challenge to you is this: Check your expectations. Reevaluate what you're asking of yourself, and make sure it aligns with the kind of life you want to lead—because you deserve to live like you give a damn about what truly matters.

23

Making Amends Is the Kindest Thing You'll Ever Do

When my kids were very young, I adopted a metaphor about "cleaning up our messes." It encompassed the act of making an actual mess, such as with their toys, and the importance of cleaning up when they were done playing. But the metaphor also meant cleaning up a mess that we made with another person in terms of hurting their feelings or making some kind of "mess" with them, and cleaning that up as well.

All of us are human, and that means we're going to screw up from time to time. We're going to say the wrong thing, do the wrong thing, or completely miss the mark with someone we care about. We're going to "make a mess." While that's a fact of life, what matters is how we clean it up—or rather, *if* we clean it up.

Here's the thing: Most of us aren't taught how to properly clean up our messes. We're not given a road map for making amends when we hurt someone, so many of us avoid it entirely. We hope the mess will just magically disappear, or maybe we convince ourselves it's not that bad. Maybe we throw out a half-assed apology, toss a quick "Sorry" over our shoulder, and call it a day. But let me tell you—doing that is like trying to hide a pizza stain on your couch with a throw pillow. It doesn't disappear. It just sits there, waiting, and eventually someone's going to notice.

Avoiding or poorly handling the cleanup doesn't just make the mess worse; it damages your relationships and your integrity. If you're not willing to own up to your mistakes, people start to notice. It chips away at the trust and connection you've built with others. It sends the message that their feelings don't matter and that keeping the peace—without actually doing the hard work of repair—is more important to you than making things right.

To be fair, making amends creates huge feelings of vulnerability. No one likes admitting they were wrong. It feels like pulling off a Band-Aid made of pride. But the truth is, vulnerability is where real connection happens. When you open yourself up, own your mess, and apologize the right way, you create space for healing—for yourself and the other person.

John M. Gottman, the relationship expert who's basically the Yoda of healthy communication, talks a lot about the importance of repair in relationships. He says it's not the absence of conflict that makes a relationship strong but rather how well you repair after the conflict happens. In fact, according to his research, the success of a relationship can often be measured by the couple's ability to make repairs after an argument or misunderstanding.[1] And here's the kicker: He's not just talking about romantic relationships. This applies to *all* your relationships—with friends, family, coworkers, anyone you care about.

So, let's break it down: You made a mess. Maybe it was something small, like a snippy comment that hurt someone's feelings. Or maybe it was something bigger—maybe you broke someone's trust or let them down in a significant way. The size of the mess doesn't really matter, but what you do next does. Cleaning it up is an act of treating your relationships like you give a damn.

What Happens If Broken Trust, Disconnection, and Guilt Are Impacting Your Life?

Now let's talk about what happens when you *don't* clean up your messes properly. First off, it chips away at your relationships. Whether you realize it or not, the people in your life are keeping track of how you show up when things go wrong. If you're the kind of person who avoids accountability, throws out weak apologies, or brushes things under the rug, you're sending a message that might read *I don't care enough about this relationship to do the hard work of repair*. You probably *do* care enough about the relationships, but by not cleaning up a mess, it can seem like you don't to the other person. Over time, that erodes trust.

When trust starts to erode, it's not always immediate or obvious. Sometimes it looks like small changes—your friend stops reaching out as much, or your partner starts pulling away emotionally. Other times, it's more dramatic—relationships fracture, people leave, or resentment builds to the point of no return. It's often because the messes weren't cleaned up.

On top of that, not addressing your mistakes can leave you feeling like crap. Whether or not you realize it, those unresolved issues create a mental and emotional load. You carry around guilt, shame, or a nagging feeling that something's "off." And let me tell you, that energy? It's heavy. It weighs you down and keeps you from being fully present in your life.

Think about it: When you know you've hurt someone but haven't made amends, it's like having a little gremlin on your shoulder, whispering in your ear, *You messed up. You're not as good a person as you think you are*. And that gremlin doesn't go away until you face the situation head-on. (Pro tip: Don't try to bribe the gremlin with snacks. I've tried. It doesn't work.)

But here's the good news: When you clean up your messes, you not only repair the relationship but also lighten your emotional load. You free yourself from guilt, shame, and disconnection. You reaffirm your commitment to living in integrity with yourself and others. Because here's what's true: Making amends is one of the kindest, most courageous things you can do—for others and for yourself.

How to Make Amends

So now that we've established the problem and how it's messing with your life, let's get to the good stuff: how to actually make amends. I'm going to give you a step-by-step guide because this is one area where the bare minimum is not enough. Half-assing an apology or skipping over key steps is only going to make things worse.

Step 1: Have Compassion for Yourself First

Before you even approach the other person, you need to have some compassion for yourself. Yes, you made a mess. Yes, you hurt someone. But guess what? You're human. You're going to screw up sometimes, and that's okay. Beating yourself up about it doesn't help anyone. What matters is that you're willing to make things right.

Start by acknowledging that making mistakes doesn't make you a bad person. It makes you a person, period. Take a deep breath and remind yourself that this is an opportunity to learn, grow, and repair.

Step 2: Express Genuine Remorse

Once you've given yourself a little grace, it's time to approach the other person. The second step in making amends is expressing genuine remorse. I want to emphasize the word *genuine* here. People can tell when you're just going through the motions or offering a quick "Sorry" to smooth things over.

A real apology starts with acknowledging the impact of your actions. It's not just about saying, "I'm sorry." It's about saying, "I understand that what I did hurt you, and I deeply regret that." You're not just apologizing for your actions—you're apologizing for the pain they caused.

Here's what this might sound like in practice:

- "I'm really sorry for what I said the other day. I realize it was hurtful, and I regret not thinking before I spoke."
- "I know I let you down by not following through on my promise. I understand how that must have affected you, and I'm genuinely sorry for that."
- "I reacted poorly earlier today, and I wish I could take back what I said. I know it was painful, and you didn't deserve that."

Notice how the focus is on the *impact* of your actions, not just the actions themselves.

Step 3: Take Responsibility

Next, it's time to take full responsibility. This is the part that can feel super vulnerable, but it's absolutely necessary. You need to own your behavior without making excuses or deflecting blame.

What you *don't* want to do is say something like, "I'm sorry you feel that way" or "I'm sorry, but if you hadn't done XYZ, I wouldn't have reacted like that." That's not an apology—that's a cop-out. A real apology is about taking ownership of what *you* did, regardless of the circumstances.

Try something like this:

- "I take full responsibility for my actions. It wasn't right for me to react the way I did, and that's on me."

- "I know I made a mistake, and I'm committed to doing better moving forward."
- "There's no excuse for how I reacted. I take full accountability for that."

By owning your behavior, you show the other person that you respect them enough to hold yourself accountable.

Step 4: Offer Restitution

After taking responsibility, it's time to offer restitution. This means finding a way to make things right. Depending on the situation, this could be as simple as asking, "What can I do to fix this?" or "How can I make it up to you?"

In some cases, restitution might involve a specific action, like rebuilding trust over time, making a tangible change in your behavior, or offering a kind gesture to show your commitment to the relationship. Whatever the case, the key is to show that you're not just apologizing with words—you're willing to back it up with action.

For example:

- "I want to rebuild trust with you, and I'm committed to doing whatever it takes to make that happen."
- "I know I hurt you, and I want to make it right. Please let me know how I can help."
- "I deeply regret the pain I've caused and am fully committed to making amends. Please tell me how I can support your healing."

Step 5: Follow Through

Finally, the last step is following through. Words are great, but actions speak louder. If you've made a commitment to change, you need to follow through on that promise. This is where trust is rebuilt—through consistent, intentional action.

If you said you'd work on being more mindful of your words, then be mindful. If you promised to be more reliable, then show up when you say you will. Your actions after the apology are just as important—if not more important—than the apology itself.

At the end of the day, making amends is about living in integrity. It's about showing people that they matter to you and that you value your relationships enough to do the hard, sometimes uncomfortable work of repair. It's not just about saying the right words; it's about embodying the commitment to growth, accountability, and connection.

When you make amends, you're not just cleaning up the mess for the other person—you're doing it for yourself. You're reinforcing your sense of self-worth, integrity, and the belief that you can face your mistakes head-on and emerge stronger. Because let's face it, we all mess up. But it's how we show up after the mess that defines who we are.

24

All You Need Isn't Love, It's Curiosity

We've all heard the idea that love is the most important thing in life. And I'll be the first to admit we all need more of it, to tap into it, to know we're made of it. Love is wonderful, no doubt. But here's the thing: If you're living without *curiosity*, you're missing a huge part of what makes life fulfilling and free. Curiosity is one of the most underrated tools in personal growth, and it doesn't get nearly enough credit. When we're not curious—about ourselves, about others, about life—we're stuck. We start to make assumptions, jump to conclusions, and tell ourselves stories that might feel real but are often not even close to the truth. And honestly, those stories are usually as wild and dramatic as a soap opera, but with way worse plot twists and zero commercial breaks to grab a snack.

Here's how this shows up in your day-to-day life: You wake up late, and immediately you're thinking, *Great, I've already screwed up today.* You're running through a mental checklist of everything you *should* have done by now, and then that sneaky inner critic starts whispering, *You're always behind. Why can't you get it together?* Boom, you've made an assumption—that you're failing, that you're not good enough—without pausing to get curious about why your day started the way it did or even if starting late really *means* anything about you.

Not having curiosity can also erode relationships. How often do you make assumptions about what your partner, your boss, or your best friend is thinking? Maybe your partner seems distant one evening, and instead of getting curious about what's going on with them, you assume it's about you. You start spiraling, creating a whole narrative in your head: *They must be upset with me. Maybe I did something wrong. What if this is the beginning of the end?* Before you know it, you're convinced your relationship is in trouble, all because you made up a story in your head instead of staying open and curious about what's really going on.

The worst part? Most of the time, these stories aren't kind. When we're not curious, we tend to assume the worst about ourselves and others. We latch on to negative beliefs, create problems that don't exist, and close ourselves off to new possibilities. Life becomes small, boxed in by these stories and assumptions that don't actually serve us.

Curiosity, though? Curiosity blows the walls off that box—like your dog spotting a squirrel during a "relaxing" walk. It's the antidote to assumptions, false narratives, and limited thinking. When you're curious, you open yourself up to new information, new perspectives, and new ways of being. You stop assuming you know all the answers and start asking more questions. That's when real growth happens—and let's be honest, it's also when you start realizing you've been wrong about a *lot* of things. (Like how kale wasn't actually the devil, and maybe your ex wasn't the *only* problem.)

What Happens If Fixed Mindsets and Fear Are Impacting Your Life?

Let's talk about how living without curiosity impacts your life, because it runs deep. A lack of curiosity isn't just a quirky habit—it's actually holding you back in ways you might not even realize.

First off, living without curiosity keeps you stuck in a fixed mindset. If you've ever heard the term *growth mindset*, you know it's all about believing you can learn, grow, and change. A fixed mindset is the opposite: It's the belief that you already know everything, or worse, that you *should* know everything. It's like walking around with a giant "I've Got This" sign when, deep down, you're googling "how to boil an egg." It's thinking that if you don't have all the answers, you're somehow flawed, broken, or behind. This mindset is paralyzing—because honestly, no one has all the answers except maybe your mom when she texts, "I told you so."

When you're not curious, you assume there's nothing new to learn—about yourself, about others, or about the world. You stop questioning things because questioning feels risky. What if the answers reveal something you don't like? What if getting curious shows you that you've been wrong? What if it forces you to change?

That's the fear talking: fear of the unknown, fear of making mistakes, fear of being vulnerable. It keeps you rigid, stuck in old beliefs and patterns that might not even serve you anymore. When you live like this, life becomes narrow. You miss out on opportunities for growth, connection, and joy because you're too afraid to ask questions, explore new ideas, or take risks.

Let's break this down a little more. In your personal life, a lack of curiosity can manifest as assumptions and miscommunication. You *assume* you know what your partner needs without asking them. You *assume* you understand your friend's motives without checking in. You *assume* you've hit your limit in a certain area of your life without even trying to push past it. All of this creates distance, misunderstandings, and unnecessary tension.

In your relationship with yourself, not being curious leads to self-judgment and shame. When something doesn't go the way you expected, instead of getting curious about what went wrong or how you can learn from it, you beat yourself up. You tell yourself stories like *I'm not good enough* or *I'll never get it right*. You make assumptions about your worth instead of staying open to the possibility that maybe, just maybe, you're doing better than you think.

At work, a lack of curiosity can hold you back from taking risks or innovating. When you're afraid to ask questions or explore new ideas, you play it safe. You stay in your lane, doing the same things over and over because it feels familiar and comfortable. But here's the thing: Comfort zones are where dreams go to die—like that houseplant you swore you'd keep alive but forgot to water for three weeks. Growth only happens when you're willing to step into the unknown, ask questions, and get curious about what's possible. Plus, stepping out of your comfort zone makes for way better stories. No one's reading a memoir titled *Stayed in My Lane: The Art of Playing It Safe*.

How to Practice Curiosity

So, how do we flip the script? How do we invite curiosity back into our lives and use it as a tool for growth, freedom, and fulfillment? I'm glad you asked, because curiosity isn't just a nice-to-have—it's essential if you want to live a life that feels rich, expansive, and true to who you are. And the good news? You can start practicing curiosity today, so you can live like you give a damn. Here's how:

Stay Open to New Perspectives

The first step to cultivating curiosity is learning to stay open. You don't have to have all the answers. In fact, it's better if you don't. Start by acknowledging that there's always something more to learn—that you're a perpetual student of life. Whether it's about yourself, the people in your life, or the world around you, there's always a new layer to uncover.

Next time you catch yourself making an assumption—about yourself, someone else, or a situation—pause. Ask yourself, *What if there's more to this story?* Instead of jumping to conclusions, get curious about what might really be going on. This small shift in perspective opens up a whole new world of possibilities.

Ask More Questions

Curiosity thrives on questions. If you want to become more curious, you've got to start asking more questions—especially the hard ones. This is a practice in turning off autopilot, slowing down, and choosing curiosity over criticism (of yourself and others). Whether it's about your own behavior or someone else's, the goal here is to shift from assumption to inquiry.

Here's a practice to learn to ask more questions and to build curiosity in your daily life:

Step 1: Start with yourself. When something goes wrong or you're feeling stuck, resist the urge to spiral or self-blame. Pause and ask yourself:
- *What can I learn from this?*
- *How can I approach this differently next time?*
- *What am I missing?*
- *Is there another way to look at this?*
- *What would Beyoncé do?*

These questions help you pivot from judgment to growth—and honestly, they bring some humor and levity to moments that can feel heavy. You don't have to have perfect answers—just asking the questions opens up space for clarity and self-compassion.

Step 2: Get curious in relationships. Instead of assuming you know what the other person is thinking or feeling (spoiler: you probably don't), start asking real questions:
- "What's going on for you?"
- "How can I support you?"
- "What do you need right now?"

These questions invite intimacy, connection, and real understanding. You'd be amazed at how much closer you can get to people when you stop trying to mind-read and just ask. And no, "What's for dinner?" doesn't count as deep connection—even if it's asked with love and a growling stomach.

Practicing curiosity is about staying open, getting honest, and being willing to not have all the answers. The more you ask, the more you learn—about yourself, the people in your life, and the world around you.

Seek New Experiences

Curiosity isn't just about asking questions—it's also about putting yourself in situations where you're forced to learn and grow. This means seeking out new experiences, trying things you've never done before, and getting comfortable with the unknown.

Start small. Try a new hobby, read a book outside your usual genre, or strike up a conversation with someone who has a different perspective than you. The point is to push yourself out of your comfort zone and invite new experiences into your life. When you do this, you're giving yourself more opportunities to be curious and learn.

Take Risks and Embrace the Process

Curiosity and risk go hand in hand. When you're curious, you're willing to take risks because you're more interested in the process than the outcome. You're not so focused on whether you succeed or fail—you're focused on what you can learn along the way.

So, take that leap. Go after the thing that scares you. Taking risks and embracing the process go hand in hand with the previous step, trying something new. Because when things don't go as planned (because let's be real, life is messy), that is your opportunity to get curious about what happened. What did you learn? What would you do differently next time? This is where real growth happens—not in the final result but in the journey.

Pay Attention to What Curiosity Brings

Finally, make a habit of reflecting on how curiosity is impacting your life. Start paying attention to the shifts that happen when you get curious. Do you feel more connected to others? Are you learning more about yourself? Are you taking more risks and feeling more alive as a result?

Curiosity creates movement and momentum. It gets you out of your head and into action. The more you practice it, the more you'll start to see evidence of what curiosity can bring: deeper relationships, personal growth, new opportunities, and a greater sense of freedom. It's not about the end result—it's about the *process* of staying open, asking questions, and learning along the way.

At the end of the day, curiosity is more than just a fun trait—it's a way of life. It's the key to breaking free from the limiting beliefs and assumptions that keep you stuck. It's the antidote to fear and judgment. Most importantly, it's your permission slip to embrace the messy, unpredictable, and wildly fascinating ride that is being human.

Because here's the truth: Curiosity isn't about having all the answers—it's about loving the questions enough to keep showing up. It's about realizing that life is less like a well-scripted movie and more like an improv show where you're both the performer and the audience. So go ahead, ask more questions, take a few risks, and let curiosity lead the way.

If anyone questions your endless curiosity, just tell them you're not nosy—you're *investigative*. Then throw in a dramatic "The truth is out there" for good measure and watch them wonder what kind of adventure you're up to next.

25

Start Acting Like the Boss of You

Self-trust comes up over and over again with the women I work with. It's like the same old story playing in the background of our lives. They come to me asking, "How do I stop second-guessing myself?" or "How do I know what the right decision is?" Time and time again, I see them looking outward for the answers, as if the solution is hiding in someone else's opinion, approval, or tarot deck. Brace yourself: It's not. It's not buried in your ex's Instagram story. It's not in the five-star Amazon review. It's definitely not in your mom's passive-aggressive advice about your life choices.

We live in a world where we've been conditioned to doubt ourselves, especially as women. We've been taught that we need to check in with everyone else—our friends, partners, family, and even strangers on the internet—before we can decide. We gather their thoughts, weigh their opinions, and then wonder why we feel so disconnected from ourselves. Why? Because we've outsourced our inner authority.

Here's how it shows up: You've got a decision to make—maybe about a career move, a relationship, or even something as simple as whether or not to sign up for a class or start a new hobby. Instead of trusting your gut and making the call, you start seeking advice from anyone with a pulse. You text your friends, you ask your mom, you scroll through social media to see if anyone else has dealt with the same issue. And with every opinion you gather, you move further away from your own inner wisdom.

The irony? A lot of the time we're asking people who have *no business* giving us advice. We ask people who are just as confused as we are—or worse, people who project their own fears and insecurities onto us. Then we wonder why we're more anxious and uncertain than when we started.

To be fair, there are some instances where gathering information or doing research on a big decision *is* helpful. But more often than not, the research and information gathering are endless and can cause more confusion and stuckness than ever, and the cycle never ends—not to mention fuels the belief that you don't trust yourself.

Here's what happens: When you rely on the counsel of others instead of trusting yourself, you end up disconnected from your own desires, instincts, and values. You become more concerned with what other people think or looking for absolute certainty that you're making the right choice than what feels right for you. This lack of self-trust is exhausting. It keeps you in a constant loop of indecision, second-guessing, and analysis paralysis. You're stuck.

You end up becoming an amateur detective, gathering evidence for why you *can't* do something. Maybe you tell yourself you don't have enough experience or that you've tried before and failed. Maybe someone else told you it's a bad idea, or someone on Reddit had a bad experience in 2008 with what you're looking into and you've latched on to that. Whatever the case, you're gathering all this "evidence" to support the narrative that you're not capable, not good enough, or not ready.

But here's the truth: The magic answers you're looking for? They're already inside of you. This may sound mysterious or even esoteric—like I'm about to hand you a crystal and chant incantations or affirmations—but it's not that complicated. You don't need someone else to tell you what to do, and you don't need more evidence of why you can't. What you need is to start trusting yourself enough to take action—even when it's scary, even when you aren't certain it will work out. Because the only way to build self-trust is through doing. Turns out, the magic was you all along (cue *The Wizard of Oz* moment).

What Happens If You Don't Focus on Being the *Boss of You*?

Let's talk about what this lack of self-trust is doing to you. I'll be honest—this part might feel a little like *Girl, that dress actually looks terrible on you*. But we need to face it head-on if we're going to make real changes.

When you don't trust yourself, it affects everything. You get stuck in indecision, afraid of making the wrong choice. You keep spinning, overthinking, asking for advice, and second-guessing yourself. It's exhausting and drains your energy, time, and mental health.

Then there's the anxiety. Looking outward for answers instead of trusting yourself leaves you unsettled. You feel like you're missing something, that others know better, or that a big mistake is looming. This creates constant, low-level anxiety. If you're like me, it can escalate to panic when you realize you've been stuck on the same decision for weeks.

But here's the real kicker: This constant lack of self-trust slowly chips away at your confidence. Every time you look to someone else for validation or permission, you're sending a message to yourself that your instincts and wisdom aren't good enough. You're reinforcing the belief that you need external approval to move forward. Over time, this erodes your confidence in a big way.

You start believing the story that you can't make good decisions on your own. You stop taking risks, stop trying new things, and stop going after what you really want because you're too afraid of failing. And when you do take action, you second-guess yourself the entire way through, never really trusting that you're on the right path.

Guess what happens next? You play small. You stay in your comfort zone because it feels safer than risking failure or making a wrong move. But here's the thing: Playing small isn't actually safe. *It's just familiar.* It's like choosing to build your house out of cardboard because you're too afraid to buy real walls—you're surviving, sure, but are you really thriving? Plus, what happens when it rains? If you stay in your small comfort zone long enough, you'll wake up one day feeling lost, unfulfilled, and wondering why your life doesn't feel like it's truly *yours*.

So, if any of this sounds familiar, it's time for a reality check. Because here's what I know for sure: You *can* trust yourself. You just have to start proving it to yourself, one decision at a time.

How to Be the Boss of You

So, how do you stop outsourcing your power to other people and start being the boss of you? How do you build that rock-solid self-trust that allows you to make decisions with confidence and move forward without constantly second-guessing yourself?

Here's the truth: Building self-trust is like building a muscle. It doesn't happen overnight, but with consistent practice, you can strengthen it over time. Here's how you start:

Take Action, Even When It's Scary and You Don't Know What to Do

The number one way to build self-trust is by taking action. You can't think your way into trusting yourself—you have to *do* your way into it. Every time you take a step toward what you're afraid of, you're proving to yourself that you can handle it. Whether it works out perfectly or not doesn't matter. What matters is that you took the step.

For example, maybe you're thinking about starting your own business or making a pivot in your career, but you're terrified of failing. Instead of sitting on the sidelines gathering more opinions, more advice, and more "evidence" of why you can't, take a small step toward it. Sign up for a class, send out a few networking emails, or start working on your business plan. Every step you take, no matter how small, will build your confidence and self-trust.

If You're Stuck Between Choices, Just Pick Something

This piece of advice tends to make people's heads explode, but hear me out. Getting stuck in indecision can be debilitating and always unproductive, but the solution doesn't have to be complicated. Sometimes the best thing you can do is just pick something and move forward. It's not about finding the perfect answer—it's about building momentum and trusting that clarity will follow action. Here are a few ways to make that happen:

- **Set a deadline.** Indecision thrives on open timelines. Give yourself a specific amount of time to decide and stick to it. Or ask a trusted friend to hold you accountable here.
- **Use the 80/20 rule.** If a choice is 80 percent "good enough," go with it. Perfection isn't necessary, and waiting for it only delays progress.
- **Recognize that no decision is perfect.** There's rarely a "right" choice, only different outcomes. Shifting your mindset to view decisions as experiments can ease the pressure. Sometimes throwing something at the wall and seeing what sticks is the best way to see what works for you.

- **Ask, *What's the worst-case scenario?*** Thinking through the worst possible outcome often reveals that it's not as bad as you fear—and most things are fixable anyway. Remember, you're resourceful and resilient!
- **Flip a coin.** It sounds silly, but even this can help. Pay attention to how you feel about the result—your gut reaction might clarify what you really want.
- **Trust that action creates clarity.** Sometimes you can only figure things out after you've made a move. Movement, even if imperfect, leads to more information and options.

Set Boundaries Around External Advice

Let me again be clear: There's nothing wrong with seeking advice from people, mentors, or experts you trust. But there's a big difference between seeking support and outsourcing your decisions. If you find yourself constantly asking for advice or validation, it's time to set some boundaries around how much input you're taking in. Because at some point, it's not research—it's just procrastination in a supercute outfit.

Before you ask someone else for advice, ask yourself, *What do I think? What feels right for me?* Practice tuning in to your own inner wisdom before you bring other people into the equation. When you do seek advice, make sure it's from people who truly understand and respect your goals—not people who are projecting their fears onto you. (Because Aunt Carol's advice about staying in your comfort zone might be coming from a place of love, but it's also coming from her recliner, where she's been bingeing *Murder, She Wrote* for the past decade.)

Start Small, Then Go Big

If you're struggling with self-trust, start small. Pick one area of your life where you feel relatively confident and begin making decisions there. As you build trust in that area, you'll start to feel more confident in other parts of your life too.

Once you've gained some momentum, start going bigger. Take on bigger challenges, make bolder decisions, and trust yourself to handle whatever comes your way. And don't forget to *celebrate*! The more you practice, the stronger your self-trust muscle will become.

At the end of the day, the only person who can make decisions for you is *you*. The magic answers you're chasing aren't tucked away in someone else's opinion, an oracle card, or unsolicited advice—they're already inside of you, like a treasure chest you forgot you buried. You have all the wisdom, courage, and insight you need to make the right choices for your life. The only thing missing? Trusting yourself enough to dig in, dust it off, and use it. So, stop waiting for a neon sign or a permission slip—your inner badass is ready when you are.

So, start being the boss of you. Stop outsourcing your power to others, stop gathering evidence for why you can't, and start proving to yourself that you can. Because I promise you—you've got this. It's all there for you. When you start to trust yourself, you start living like you give a damn.

Conclusion

This Is What It Means to Give a Damn

If you've made it this far, you've already done something so many people never do: You've chosen to look at your life—*really* look at it—and ask yourself, *What needs to change?* That's not small. That's not surface. That's revolutionary.

Living like you give a damn isn't about being perfect or even close to perfect. It's not about "arriving." It's not about checking off a neat little list of personal development goals and then kicking your feet up with a green juice like you've figured it all out.

It's about showing up. Day after day. Moment after moment.

It's about telling the truth when it would be easier to lie, especially to yourself.

It's about holding your own damn hand when things feel messy and unfixable.

It's about remembering—again and again—that you get to choose how you respond, who you become, and what you believe about yourself.

Some days you'll do it with fire and fury. Some days you'll do it with tears in your eyes and no clean underwear to put on after you slept through your alarm. Doesn't matter. You're doing it.

The twenty-five bold moves in this book? They're not a checklist. They're a tool kit. They're invitations. They're proof that you can live a life that feels like yours. A life you're not apologizing for. A life where you trust yourself, back yourself, and believe—deep down—that you are worthy of the damn good stuff.

And let's be real—this work? It's not linear. There is no finish line. You might circle back to the same lesson more than once (hello, boundaries and shame). That doesn't mean you've failed. It means you're still in the game. And that's the point.

You're going to disappoint people. You're going to walk away from things that once defined you. You're going to grieve, and rage, and second-guess yourself, and still you'll keep going. You'll get better at knowing who you are and what you want. You'll get braver. You'll soften in all the right places and stand taller in the ones that matter most.

So here's my final ask of you:

Keep going. Keep choosing yourself. Keep getting up after you've fallen down.

Even when it's hard. Especially when it's hard.

You don't need to have it all figured out. You just need to give enough of a damn to keep showing up, one bold move at a time.

And babe? You've already started.

Thank you for trusting me with your time, your attention, and maybe even a piece of your life while you've read this book. That's not lost on me—I'm incredibly grateful you let me walk alongside you in this chapter of your growth.

If you want to keep going—and I hope you do—head over to andreaowen.com/LLYGAD for special free bonuses and ways to stay connected to this work. We're just getting started.

Notes

Introduction
1 *I Ching*, trans. Richard Wilhelm and Cary F. Baynes, Bollingen Series 19 (Princeton, NJ: Princeton University Press, 1967), 32–39.

Chapter 4: Have a Fierce Throwdown with Fear
1 Steven Pressfield, *The War of Art: Break Through the Blocks and Win Your Inner Creative Battles* (New York: Black Irish Entertainment, 2002).

Chapter 13: Rush the Net
1 Ian Robertson, *How Confidence Works: The New Science of Self-Belief* (London: Bantam Press, 2021).

Chapter 16: People Will Judge You, and Sometimes They're Just Not That Into You
1 Ethan Kross, Marc G. Berman, Walter Mischel, Edward E. Smith, and Tor D. Wager, "Social Rejection Shares Somatosensory Representations with Physical Pain," *Proceedings of the National Academy of Sciences* 108, no. 15 (2011): 6270–75, doi.org/10.1073/pnas.1102693108.
2 Meghan L. Meyer, Kipling D. Williams, and Naomi I. Eisenberger, "Why Social Pain Can Live On: Different Neural Mechanisms Are Associated with Reliving Social

and Physical Pain," *PLOS One* 10, no. 6 (2015): e0128294, doi.org/10.1371/journal.pone.0128294.

Chapter 17: Be Impractical

1 Barbara Sher, *Refuse to Choose! Use All of Your Interests, Passions, and Hobbies to Create the Life and Career of Your Dreams* (Emmaus, PA: Rodale Books, 2006).

Chapter 18: Whatever You Think You Are Will Be Your Truth

1 *Mean Girls*, directed by Mark Waters, screenplay by Tina Fey (Los Angeles: Paramount Pictures, 2004).

Chapter 23: Making Amends Is the Kindest Thing You'll Ever Do

1 John M. Gottman and Joan DeClaire, *The Relationship Cure: A Five-Step Guide to Strengthening Your Marriage, Family, and Friendships* (New York: Harmony Books, 2001).

About the Author

Andrea Owen is a life coach, author, and speaker who helps high-achieving women let go of what's holding them back so they can live with confidence and courage and feel truly alive. Her bestselling books—including *How to Stop Feeling Like Sh*t*—have been translated into twenty languages and have inspired thousands of women around the world to step into their power. Known for her signature mix of hype-girl energy and deep, transformational coaching, Andrea brings humor, heart, and relatability to everything she does. She lives in North Carolina.

Also by Andrea Owen

Make Some Noise

How to Stop Feeling Like Sh*t

RAISING READERS
Books Build Bright Futures

Dear Reader,

We'd love your attention for one more page to tell you about the crisis in children's reading, and what we can all do.

Studies have shown that reading for fun is the **single biggest predictor of a child's future life chances** – more than family circumstance, parents' educational background or income. It improves academic results, mental health, wealth, communication skills, ambition and happiness.[1]

The number of children reading for fun is in rapid decline. Young people have a lot of competition for their time. In 2024, 1 in 10 children and young people in the UK aged 5 to 18 did not own a single book at home.[2]

Hachette works extensively with schools, libraries and literacy charities, but here are some ways we can all raise more readers:

- Reading to children for just 10 minutes a day makes a difference
- Don't give up if children aren't regular readers – there will be books for them!
- Visit bookshops and libraries to get recommendations
- Encourage them to listen to audiobooks
- Support school libraries
- Give books as gifts

There's a lot more information about how to encourage children to read on our website: **www.RaisingReaders.co.uk**

Thank you for reading.

---

[1] OECD, '21st-Century Readers: Developing Literacy Skills in a Digital World', 2021, https://www.oecd.org/en/publications/21st-century-readers_a83d84cb-en.html

[2] National Literacy Trust, 'Book Ownership in 2024', November 2024, https://literacytrust.org.uk/research-services/research-reports/book-ownership-in-2024

books to help you live a good life

Join the conversation and tell us how you live a #goodlife

🐦 @yellowkitebooks
f YellowKiteBooks
P Yellow Kite Books
📷 YellowKiteBooks